Composers on Composing for Choir

Also available from GIA Publications, Inc.
Edited by Mark Camphouse

Composers on Composing for Band, Volume One
James Barnes
Timothy Broege
Mark Camphouse
David Gillingham
David R. Holsinger
Karel Husa
Timothy Mahr
W. Francis McBeth
Robert Sheldon
Jack Stamp
Frank Ticheli

Composers on Composing for Band, Volume Two
James Curnow
Johan de Meij
Julie Giroux
Donald Grantham
Robert Jager
Pierre La Plante
David Maslanka
Philip Sparke
Eric Whitacre
Dana Wilson

Composers on Composing for Band, Volume Three
Andrew Boysen, Jr.
Edward Gregson
Samuel R. Hazo
Quincy C. Hilliard
Joseph Willcox Jenkins
Stephen Melillo
Roger Nixon
Jared Spears
Jan Van der Roost
John Zdechlik

Composers
on **Composing**
for **Choir**

edited by **Tom Wine**

david n. **Childs**
rené **Clausen**
libby **Larsen**
morten **Lauridsen**
kirke **Mechem**
james **Mulholland**
john **Rutter**
z. randall **Stroope**
andré **Thomas**
gwyneth **Walker**

GIA Publications, Inc.
Chicago

Composers on Composing for Choir
Edited by Tom Wine
GIA Publications, Inc.
7404 S. Mason Ave., Chicago 60638
Copyright © 2007 GIA Publications, Inc.
Printed in the United States of America

G-7110
ISBN-13: 978-1-57999-664-2

Cover design: Martha Chlipala
Book layout: Robert Sacha

www.giamusic.com

Table of Contents

Introduction

Tom Wine

According to Thomas Edison, "Success is 10 percent inspiration and 90 percent perspiration." The composers in *Composers on Composing for Choir* bring a tremendous work ethic to their craft. For aspiring choral composers this book offers exceptional insights into the creative process, and for conductors this book provides a glimpse into the creative mind.

Inspired by a similar book series featuring composers of band literature compiled and edited by Mark Camphouse, this book's intended audience includes both conductors and aspiring composers. The format of the book asks each composer to offer their perspectives on the following topics:

A. Biography: a formal background as well as personal anecdotes
B. The Creative Process: the inspiration behind the music
C. The Relationship Between Text and Music
D. Views from the Composer to the Conductor Pertaining to Score Study and Preparation: advice for performing the composer's repertoire
E. The Relationship Between the Composer and the Commissioning Party: a how-to manual
F. Views on the Teaching of Composition and How to Mentor the Young Composer
G. Individuals Who Were Especially Influential in My Development and Career

As a reader, you may choose to read each chapter in order from beginning to end, or you might find it interesting to follow each topic as it is presented by the composers.

From the composer's perspective, music is an idealized representation of notes and rests designed to evoke an emotional awakening in the performer and ultimately the audience. Jazz trumpet player Miles Davis is famous for saying "Don't play what's there. Play what's not there." The purpose of this book is to help illuminate some of the intent behind the composer's vision and help the conductor interpret the music better for the ensemble and for the listener.

Each composer in the book was asked to suggest a list of ten pieces appropriate for future study by choral conductors. The pieces suggested in this book represent music that has proved worthy of repeat performances and has stood the test of time. These pieces deserve continued study because each visit with the musical score and each performance will awaken new nuances for the conductor, the performer, and the audience. André Thomas suggested that every student of choral music should know a model example of a hymn, a folk song, and an art song as well as the choral masterpieces. The student of choral music (whether composer or conductor) will find valuable reference materials for their development in this field of endeavor.

I would also like to thank my editors, Alec Harris and Elizabeth Bentley, for their guidance during this process. I would like to thank all of the composers who gave so generously of their

time and talents to make this book possible. Finally, I would like
to thank Mary, John, and Jenny for their support.

david n. Childs

A. Biography

D avid N. Childs was born in 1969 in Nelson, New Zealand. He has a bachelor's degree in composition and musicology from Canterbury University, Christchurch, New Zealand; a master of music degree in conducting from the Florida State University–Tallahassee; and a doctorate of musical arts degree from Louisiana State University. Childs currently serves as assistant professor of choral studies at the Blair School of Music at Vanderbilt University in Nashville.

He is music director of the Vanderbilt Opera Theater program, having conducted performances of W. A. Mozart's *The Magic Flute*, Giocomo Puccini's *Gianni Schicchi*, Gian Carlo Menotti's *Amelia Goes to the Ball* and *The Telephone*, Harvey Schmidt's *Fantasticks*, Gilbert and Sullivan's *The Pirates of Penzance*, Leonard Bernstein's *Trouble in Tahiti*, and Stephen Sondheim's *A Little Night Music*.

Childs's primary conducting teachers include Kenneth Fulton, André Thomas, and Professor Rodney Eichenberger. He has received additional instruction from Helmuth Rilling while working as a master class conductor at the Oregon Bach Festival. Childs is an active clinician and adjudicator in the United States, working at the grade school, college, and community levels. He has conducted all-state and honor choirs in Tennessee, Virginia, Mississippi, Louisiana, Oregon, Alabama, Florida, and Georgia. In addition to conducting and teaching, Childs has more than thirty-five choral works in print with Santa Barbara Music Publishers and Alliance Music. His compositions are frequently performed at state festivals and workshops and at ACDA state, regional, and national conventions.

***

Without a doubt meeting my adopted father was the most significant musical (and emotional) event in my life, and it happened when I was a boy of about ten. My medicine-practicing (birth) father and mother had separated (and subsequently divorced) some three years earlier, and the day we met David Christopher Childs—our stepfather to be—in 1978, life took on a new and exciting perspective for us all.

My stepfather's title was organist and master of the choristers at Christchurch Cathedral in New Zealand. He married into the family when I was nearly eleven, and soon after he encouraged me to begin formal piano lessons. Aside from the practical advantages of having a musical father (proofing my music theory homework, helping me with particularly difficult musical problems), I learned much from simply observing him and by immersing myself in his professional world whenever possible. Although I was never actually a boy chorister of his, I nevertheless attended many services at the cathedral and frequently served as an acolyte or crucifer. It was from such a vantage point that I learned to appreciate organ and choral music and even became a regular "page-turner" for my father's organ recitals. (That was until, during one recital, I inadvertently stepped on a couple of the lowest pedal notes!)

My years in the Christchurch Cathedral cultivated in me a passion for all styles and forms of choral music, although much of what I heard was of English descent. My father was a very fine conductor, and so through observation, osmosis, and conducting in front of a mirror (to some of the finest orchestras in the world— limited only to the extent of my father's LP record collection), my informal conducting instruction began. Not long after that I decided this was the particular path I wished to pursue. I had the opportunity to conduct a small, sixteen-voice chamber choir at high school, which further whetted my conducting appetite, and from that moment on I never looked back. My father was always very supportive and encouraging of me, although he was anxious that I might lose my passion for music should I decide to pursue a career as a professional musician—one that was fraught with financial challenges among many other hurdles.

Music seemed to come naturally to me—as if it were destined to play a significant role in my life. The curriculum at Burnside High School (in Christchurch, New Zealand) included instruction in music theory, harmony, composition, analysis, history, and ear training. If students wished to participate in ensembles (which was expected of all academic music students) they had to do so as an extracurricular activity. Choir, orchestra, band, and chamber groups were not part of the formal musical instruction we received. I did well enough in my other academic disciplines, but I flourished in music. I relished composition, theory, and performance, which were all taught as part of the New Zealand music curriculum for thirteen- to seventeen-year-olds (approximately grades 8–12). There were times when my "other-subject" teachers would turn a blind eye so I could sneak off to practice on the new grand piano in the assembly hall. It quickly became evident that a career in music was inevitable for me.

My father was an extremely well-rounded musician. During the tercentenary celebrations of J. S. Bach's birth in 1985, he adeptly improvised a long organ prelude and fugue on "Happy Birthday"—in the Baroque style. I remember being so impressed and very proud of him. Once I asked my father to write me a couple of piano pieces while on vacation in a beautiful part of Bank's Peninsular—about a two-hour drive out of Christchurch (in the South Island of New Zealand). We were on holiday, away from a piano, yet he quickly penned two small works for me, including the *Takamatua Waltz*, named after a particular inlet in which we were staying. (Takamatua is a Mâori, or native New Zealand, name.) I was thoroughly impressed that he could compose something so meaningful completely in his head. Events such as these continued to stimulate my infatuation with music and guided me in my decision to write music of my own.

My earliest formal composing experience occurred at Burnside High School in Christchurch. I feel extremely fortunate that Burnside participated in the Composer-In-Schools program, which appointed nationally recognized itinerant composers to teach the craft to music students at several area schools. At my particular school, Dorothy Buchanan was charged with the task of introducing fundamental composition techniques to the "third-formers" (equivalent to North American high school freshmen) and to instruct the senior music students at more technically advanced levels. To most educators in the United States this approach would seem somewhat unusual and exceptional. Few school systems in the world offer such specialization so early in school life, and I am still most grateful for this privilege. From my early teens I explored a myriad of compositional techniques, and I was encouraged to compose in all manner of styles. I vividly recall setting some choral pieces in hymn style when I was fifteen.

It was at this pivotal moment in my musical life that I seriously contemplated studying composition at the university level.

At the university, however, I became discouraged by what I considered a narrow-minded teaching style by the composition professors. It was my impression that students were strongly encouraged to write in a restrictive postmodern style I perceived as soulless, stark, and pretentiously academic. Paradoxically, I was fascinated by the study of works by twentieth-century composers such as John Cage, Milton Babbit, Terry Riley, Arnold Schonberg, and Philip Glass. I admittedly enjoyed experimenting with various tonal languages, but ultimately I was too committed to my own style and strongly resisted the establishment of the time.

My studies in composition at the university lasted a mere two years, and it was not until almost six years later that I began writing again. My reentry into composition was more for pragmatic reasons than anything else. The high school ensembles I was directing at the time required new music, and, rather than pay exorbitant shipping and handling fees to import sheet music from the USA (the exchange rate was not in favor of the New Zealand dollar at the time), I simply decided to give composing another shot. I wrote three choral pieces and, on a whim, decided to submit them to several music houses for publishing consideration.

I naively failed to investigate publishing protocol and promptly mailed off ten packets of my new compositions to various publishing houses in the United States. It takes about six to seven days for mail to reach the Americas, and exactly one week later I received a fax from Barbara Harlow, president of Santa Barbara Music Publishing, stating she wanted to publish them. The very next day I received a facsimile from Warner Brothers, who also wanted to publish one of the three pieces—

"Set Me as a Seal." To my horror and embarrassment they had already put a contract in the mail. I promptly placed a long-distance call to them apologizing profusely for my misjudgment. They were very understanding and diplomatically explained to me the correct procedure for future manuscript submissions.

B. The Creative Process

The first place I look for inspiration is the text. Locating a suitable text can be one of the most time-consuming aspects of choral composition, yet I believe it is one of the most important. Copious hours may be spent reading poetry books or searching through poetry Web sites. I read as many poems as I possibly can until I find one that resonates with me. Melodies, harmonies, and rhythms metamorphose out of the poems, and an important part of my creative process necessitates spending quiet time with the text—letting it speak to me. This text-driven process ultimately determines the entire form and tone of the new composition.

Although I do not have a favorite poet, I do enjoy the writings of Sara Teasdale and Emily Dickinson, and I have set several of their poems to music. Vernacular biblical passages as well as sacred Latin texts have also been favorite writing sources. Very rarely and with great reluctance do I agree to set a text someone else has chosen, an issue that occasionally arises when commissioned to write works. I personally consider it fraudulent to set a text that does not speak to you and move you on a personal level. Never have I attempted to set preexisting music to a poem. The very concept seems anathema to composing and to the creative process. I do, however, know a handful of composers who have used such a process—including the

Australian-New Zealand band Crowded House—an approach that has clearly proved very successful for them.

Once I have selected and spent time with a poem, I attempt to create a rough plan or compositional structure based upon the form of the poem. Part of this process involves identifying the dramatic and static moments of the poem and deciding how to present these movements using a musical approach. When *painting* text, there is a real danger that the musical writing will become too obvious and clichéd. It is tempting to set every ecstatic line of text in a dramatic fashion, but if executed without subtlety and care the music may become trite and predictable as a result.

The overall tone of the poem will suggest a major or minor key (or keys) and determine whether I use a quick tempo with energetic, complex rhythms and quickly changing harmonies or a more sedate approach with a slower harmonic rhythm. More specifically, smaller, noteworthy events in the poem require attention. For example, a "turn" in the text (either dramatic or subtle) may perhaps invite some musical treatment as well as a shift in musical nuance. With regard to timbre, many texts are perfectly suited to SATB settings, but other poems are clearly gender specific, demanding a setting for men's, women's, or children's voices.

Throughout this initial phase in the compositional process, it is important that I be removed from the piano. The inner ear must be given a chance to devise melodies or motifs without the interference of a musical crutch such as a keyboard. I have written some of my most successful music on a noisy bus! On other occasions sitting on a quiet park bench has proved conducive to my creative process. The ability to create melodies and harmonies in one's head and to be able to transcribe such ideas onto manuscript without relying on a musical instrument is one of the most mysterious and wonderful aspects of being a composer.

Only when I have completed the melodic, tonal, and structural framework will I go to the piano. Typically I organize the choral parts first while an accompaniment (if there is one) quietly ferments in my subconscious. I might write out some harmonies away from the keyboard, but I ultimately end up working out the raw harmonic material at the piano. I grew up playing the piano, so it is no surprise that I consider the accompaniment to be an integral part of many of my compositions. It's important to me that the accompaniment be strong and reflective of the text as it is in the lieder of Schubert and Schumann, not simply an afterthought.

Unlike several composers, I have yet to develop a composing routine of my own. My daily teaching schedules are so varied it is almost impossible to set aside a common time for composing each and every day. Some weeks I am involved in late-night opera rehearsals, out of town, or simply get caught up in office work. As a result I have been most unsuccessful at establishing a composing regimen. The result is erratic periods of productivity, which sometimes lead to a composing hiatus of many months. Most of my composing is done in a compressed time frame spanning a few weeks at a time.

C. The Relationship Between Text and Music

At any point on a given day, musical melodies will slip in and out of my consciousness, sometimes manifesting themselves in the form of fresh, original airs, while at other times I endure inane repetitious motifs from existing (not usually my own) compositions. When I manage to stifle thoughts of schoolwork, dinner menus, or the next meeting, the resultant "space" in my head frequently becomes occupied with melodies, harmonies, and new compositional ideas. Mostly—whether original or not—I consider such musical thoughts background or white noise. They occur frequently and inconveniently, and more often than not it is simply impracticable to write them down. On rare occasions melodies and harmonies are catchy enough to record on manuscript; sometimes I am forced to do so in the middle of the night. Usually, however, I allow them to "appear" when I am ready for them to do so—during organized blocks of "composition time."

Almost always, however, the music worth capturing has been the result of a poem or specific text I have been working with that I have allowed to "ferment" over time. Typically the text becomes the primary catalyst for the entire compositional process. Frequently, I have to allow fleeting musical thoughts to come and go, as beautiful and as inspiring as some of them are in the mind's ear, otherwise I would be constantly distracted. This is one of the most difficult disciplines required of a composer—to sift the wheat from the chaff, so to speak. I long ago learned the importance of letting most musical "head noise" go, allowing it to "play out" in my mind even when I have no intention of transcribing it into musical form.

One of the many self-criticisms I have is that much of my compositional oeuvre is slow. Probably 80 percent of my compositions have a metronome marking of quarter note = 80 or less. There are relatively few quick-tempo pieces in my repertoire. My tendency to write in the slower style stems from my attraction to romantic and deeply moving texts that deal with pivotal humanistic themes and powerful emotions such as death and unrequited love.

For reasons I cannot fully explain, I am especially adept at writing intense, yearning, or sad themes and motifs. I recognize how powerful music is in its ability to move and to heal people, to reach into a person's psyche, and to resonate intimately with basic thoughts and feelings. I understand and relate to the rawest of painful human emotions possibly because I have experienced firsthand the unexpected and gut-wrenching death of a beloved parent and the effective loss of another parent through divorce when I was seven. Loss, especially in those formative childhood years, had a profound effect on me, and I truly believe such experiences have manifested themselves in much of my music. It makes reasonable sense—some childhood memories are simply too powerful to erase. Those we tend to subjugate eventually manifest themselves in other forms, occupying precious space in our psyches. I believe this is particularly true for many successful artists in all fields. I, for one, found great solace in music from an early age—even as a child I recognized its ability to provoke powerful emotional responses from within me.

Much of the sacred music I have composed is in the Latin motet style ("O magnum mysterium," "O nata lux," "Salve Regina," "O vos omnes," et. al), which I find odd because I have tenuous Roman Catholic roots at best. For reasons I cannot explain, the Latin works appeal to me more than any other genre of music.

My self-categorized "vernacular sacred style" draws upon biblical texts almost without exception, although no particular version or book of the Bible is preferred. In the past I have set texts from the Song of Solomon and the books of Ruth and Jeremiah as well as some popular verses from the Book of John. Depending on the text and on the tone I wish to create, I will source passages from a variety of bibles, from the traditional King

James Bible to the New International Version. More often than not I paraphrase biblical texts drawn from more than one original source. As appealing as the outdated, archaic language of the King James Bible is to me, I prefer to set a text in a more modern, succinct, and meaningful way so as to create works that have a broader appeal to contemporary congregations.

Some texts pose an extraordinary challenge because of their unusual meter, content, or language. This is true in several of my secular works, including the *Two Songs of Reflection* with texts by the Italian poet Umberto Saba, where the challenge was to capture the textual nuances of a foreign language in an appropriately reflective musical manner. Although I have yet to set poetry by an American modernist, the works of E. E. Cummings are particularly fascinating to me. Poems of postmodernists like Kenneth Rexroth can pose even more challenges, although some composers relish the challenge of setting obscure or unusual and irregular texts. This frequently results in a freer work, demonstrating a more uninhibited exploration of compositional forms and styles. I occasionally find myself trapped into writing in one particular style, using a comfortable, yet predictable language that is neither exploratory nor refreshing. Choosing a poem of an unusual or different style, genre, or period can certainly lead to the examination of new musical ideas.

D. Views from the Composer to the Conductor Pertaining to Score Study and Preparation

Perhaps somewhat atypically, I do not have strong opinions about how my works should be interpreted. Unless a conductor or an ensemble completely ignores the fundamental musical indications in the score, such as metronome markings and dynamics, I am comfortable with allowing the performers a certain amount of latitude to interpret the music themselves. To me, this reinforces the idea that composing is a collaborative effort, one that requires the cooperation and dialogue of both parties for a successful and satisfactory performance. The composer must allow conductors some freedom or license to interpret the music based on their prior knowledge, musical tastes, and emotional experiences. It is futile to attempt recreating the music as it first appeared in the mind's ear of the composer—where it existed in perhaps the most perfect state it ever was and ever will be again.

I believe composers hear in their "mind's ear" pieces of theirs performed without flaws, with perfect intonation, precise dynamics, and detailed articulations. A live performance (or even a recording) can never match such a standard, and there is little point in chasing an impossible ideal. It is unlikely that any composer could ever perfectly recreate his or her own works, and one would think the composer has an advantage over most! People respond and react to music in different ways. Performers will likely never experience the exact emotions, thoughts and feelings the composers had during the process of writing a work, but they will undoubtedly respond with similar feelings and correlating emotional responses based on personal experiences.

When beginning the process of composition, I will usually give careful consideration to tonal style. One such tonal style of mine may be categorized as a more traditional sacred, accompanied genre for modern day worship or for public school choirs (the vernacular sacred style mentioned earlier). Works in this style tend to be written for SATB choir with a piano accompaniment and frequently include an obbligato instrumental line. They are relatively straightforward and require little intensive rehearsing, which appeals to most church and school choirs.

The second style is typified by the larger, more challenging *a cappella* works. Most of my Latin motets fall into this category, in which I typically use divisi part writing, frequent disjunct melodic intervals, and rich, complex vocal harmonies. I believe that this style grew out of my intense appreciation for the works of Francis Poulenc, Benjamin Britten, and Ralph Vaughan Williams, as well as from the influence of the Anglican service music I heard in my youth.

The third style is more ethereal and impressionistic and is easily the least common or prolific of the three and uses more dissonance, harmonic instability, and spontaneity than the first two categories. For example, in the "Sonetto di Primavera" from *Two Songs of Reflection,* I use this freer compositional technique rather than the motet style.

On paper I record my musical thoughts as best I can, but the nature of composing is such that you cannot always exactly transcribe your musical ideas or thoughts as you idealize them in your head. Nor is it possible, or even reasonable, to control the performance of such a work once it reaches the domain of the choral community. As a composer and conductor I appreciate the challenges directors and singers face in recreating my pieces with the intent and exactitude I had in mind when writing them. I believe it important to encourage directors and ensembles to put their *own* mark or stamp on the piece. I like to be able to sit back and enjoy a performance without being too judgmental about the final product. Naturally, the composer will always evaluate the technical aspects of the performance on some level, but I try—as best as possible—to free myself to listen to and enjoy the music without engaging the critic in me.

If I could make one suggestion to conductors, it would be to consider more carefully the tempos of every piece, then to sing and play through the quickest rhythms in the music so that the most descriptive and poignant words are not rushed. The speed of the music must always be reflective of the text. An inclusion of a subtle sense of rubato is to be encouraged, especially in pieces such as "Weep No More." There are many ways to interpret music, and I encourage performers to enjoy the learning and interpretive process without becoming too concerned about what may be right or wrong.

E. The Relationship Between the Composer and the Commissioning Party

I have learned—mostly through trial and error—that the most important ingredients in the commissioning process are honesty and candor. Many people from all walks of life still feel a certain degree of awkwardness and are reluctant to discuss money. This is an unfortunate aspect of society, as money plays a pivotal role in all that we do. When I first began accepting commissions I must confess that I was equally awkward about discussing financial details with the commissioning party. I decided a new approach was necessary.

The following is a simplified version of the process by which I now operate: 1) a party offers to commission a work; 2) fees are discussed and agreed upon; 3) details of the composition (such as composing forces, completion date, accompaniment, duration and occasionally text) are discussed and agreed upon; 4) a contract is mailed out to the commissioning party, signed, and returned to the composer with a deposit; 5) the composition process begins. Upon completion and receipt of the final work, the remaining payment is due.

Although some readers may be questioning my inclusion of money before anything else, it is important to remember that composing is a business for most—if not all—composers. I have been burned a couple of times because I did not get a signed contract and a deposit before commencing work on a composition. Composers rightfully consider commissions part of their livelihoods in the same manner small business operators or proprietors do. It is essential that composers are completely candid, honest, and professional throughout the entire process, and this involves the frank discussion of commissioning fees. The commissioning process necessitates a mutually comfortable yet professional approach from both the composer and commissioning party. Neither party should proceed unless both are 100 percent comfortable. Hypothetically, if a commissioning party insisted that I compose a piece to a text that did not resonate with me, I would likely politely decline the commission rather than proceed.

As outlined in point three, it is important to set basic parameters for the composition early in the process. This includes the discussion of voicing; the ability of the group (hence the difficulty level of the piece); the general length of the work; whether it is to be accompanied or sung *a cappella*; the date by which the piece is to be performed; rights to the first recording; an allowance for the copying of the work; whether a dedication is to be included below the title; and some text possibilities. Sometimes the events may occur in a different order. The text may be the catalyst for a commission, or it may even be the final parameter discussed and decided upon. Generally composers prefer being given some latitude in choosing texts. Only once was I asked to set a particular text, which fortunately was one I already liked. In any event, composers will probably not set a text to which they do not respond well.

Having been charged with the task of finding suitable possibilities for a text I will immediately go to several collections of poetry books for inspiration, or to the many poetry Web sites available. Typically I then send the commissioning party six to twelve favorites and request that they select from these texts. It is preferable to include the commissioning party in any way possible—to give them the opportunity to participate in the decision-making process. This is usually appreciated, although some clients may occasionally feel a little overwhelmed when making such a decision.

Composing a piece with knowledge of a choir's particular voice or sound is important. I try to write each commissioned work with the choir's final performance in mind because it is essential that the composition closely match the style and capabilities of the ensemble. If the final product is impossibly difficult to perform, you have likely wasted people's time and money. Compact discs or informal recordings are often available and provide a good opportunity to ascertain a choir's limits and strengths. One quickly gets a feel for the choir; for the tessitura, sound quality, vocal technique, etc. I am convinced the commissioning party greatly appreciates this custom design approach to the composition. It is essential that both parties leave the process completely satisfied, as this may pave the way for future commissions.

F. Views on the Teaching of Composition and How to Mentor the Young Composer

The study of the art of composition is one that is continual and one that necessitates corollary studies in other musical domains. Composers must learn to crawl before they can walk and to walk before they can run, and an essential part of learning to write involves the mastery of form, harmony, and counterpoint. I am convinced these three skills stand above all others. Once one has mastered part writing and fugue and has studied basic binary form and the more complex sonata or rondo forms, etc., an appropriate foundation is laid out. Further studies should include the orchestration and text setting.

With regard to the actual teaching of composition, I believe it is imperative to *guide* rather than to *instruct*. Students should be encouraged to record on manuscript any ideas they might have, even if they consider them trifling or insignificant. These might comprise seemingly unrelated short motifs, or they may be longer, developed phrases. At this germinal stage, the large, structural picture is not so important.

Once a rudimentary form or structure has been shaped and enough harmonic and melodic material has been written, the student should be encouraged to begin building. The compositional instructor should not expect a skyscraper; many impressive buildings have been small. As long as the composition has form and structure and holds together, it should be regarded as legitimate. Composing is a rite of passage. Very few composers are brilliant in their high school or college years. The art of composition does not occur overnight. It is a continually evolving growth process that requires nurturing and a certain amount of maturation.

It is essential that students of composition broaden their listening and score study experiences, carefully studying every style from medieval to modern. The reason Mozart and Mendelssohn (among countless others) studied the music of J. S. Bach is because it contains many important harmonic, textural, and structural elements worthy of emulating. These are among the reasons we continue to study his compositions to this day.

Perhaps the most important aspect of the composition teacher's role is to encourage students, to open young composers' minds without forcing them to compose in any particular style. Allowing students to find their own compositional language by guiding them to study and listen to as many styles and genres as possible is an imperative role of the instructor.

G. Individuals Who Were Especially Influential in My Development and Career

Early in life my greatest influence was, without a doubt, my step-father, David Christopher Childs. He was such an inspiration, supporter, friend, mentor, and a patient father—a true academic and musical genius as well as a kind soul. I looked up to him and respected him above any other adult, and I often reflect on how I could have turned out to be just an average musician without his influence and input.

My stepfather occasionally programmed Latin motets in the weekly or Sunday services, but my recollection is that the majority of service music his cathedral choir sang stemmed from the English school, including works by Herbert Sumsion, Charles Villiers Stanford, Herbert Howells, Hubert Parry, and Arthur Wood, to name a few. Without a doubt such exposure to this important and sublime genre of sacred music affected me profoundly, and it continues to have an impact on me to this day. Listening to my father's well-trained choir during my teenage years was a wonderful way to learn the importance of pure vowel sounds, accurate intonation and dynamic range, and compositional style.

Dorothy Buchanan is one of New Zealand's most well-known and respected composers. During my high school years she was given the role of the itinerant composition teacher—a job that entailed much traveling and visits to numerous schools in our area. Included on her list was my school—Burnside High School in Christchurch, New Zealand. Over the course of my third-form school year, Dorothy worked with us on compositional style and technique for only one hour per week. She was a wonderfully kind, patient teacher who left an indelible impression on our thirteen-year-old minds.

I recall at age eighteen being hosted at the home of one of New Zealand's finest composers—Douglas Mews. He spent several evenings with me enticing melodic fragments and ideas from me, the reluctant, shy, and highly self-critical musician I was at the time. I greatly appreciated the fact he did not force, criticize, or have unrealistic expectations of me. To this day I clearly remember those informal lessons, and although Douglas Mews died some years ago, I am deeply grateful for the amount of time he chose to spend guiding me over the course of that brief week.

From the moment I was first published with Santa Barbara Music Publishing, the president, Barbara Harlow, has been wonderfully supportive and encouraging. I owe much of my success to her and her wonderful music company.

H. Ten Choral Works All Choral Conductors at All Levels Should Study

This would have been a much easier task had I been asked to select 100 choral works to study. The ten I have chosen are almost exclusively sacred or based on biblical events, which is no coincidence when one considers the significance of choral music in faith and worship over the centuries. They are all large major works, although I could have easily included smaller choral mas-

terpieces such as any one of the J. S. Bach motets, the William
Byrd three-, four- or five-part Masses, or Benjamin Britten's
Rejoice in the Lamb. The large works seem to have more scope for
young conductors to study.

1. The J. S. Bach Mass in B minor and the St. John and St.
   Matthew Passions: of these three, if I were to pick only one
   Bach, it would be the *Passion according to St. Matthew*. Both
   passions are incredibly moving and powerful. All three are
   truly monumental works.
2. Franz Joseph Haydn's *Creation* was very progressive and
   ahead of its time. It is very expressive and contains many
   programmatic elements that other works of the era do not.
3. Johannes Brahms's Requiem.
4. Benjamin Britten's *War Requiem*. I have always been a fan of
   Britten. This work is one of the most powerful he ever wrote.
   The interpolation of English poems by the World War I poet
   Wilfred Owens and the traditional Latin Requiem Mass text
   is incredibly moving—an ingenious stroke of brilliance on
   Britten's part.
5. Edward Elgar's *Dream of Gerontius*.
6. Felix Mendelssohn's *Elijah*.
7. The W. A. Mozart Mass in C Minor. This work is arguably
   Mozart's most outstanding choral/orchestral composition.
8. Igor Stravinsky's *Symphony of Psalms*.
9. The Giuseppe Verdi Requiem.
10. William Walton's *Belshazzar's Feast*.

I. The Future of Choral Music

Wherever compositional styles may take us in the next fifty years
or so, I am confident that the tradition of choral music is going
to continue to grow at an incredibly healthy rate. There will

always be room in the oeuvre of choral music for a variety of styles—from the more accessible tonal compositions to the challenging avant-garde atonal, polytonal, or nontraditional harmonic works. As exciting and refreshing as modern choral music can be, I do not see a large tonal shift toward atonality, minimalism, or serialism only because the capabilities of the human voice, especially for young singers, limit the successful performance of such pieces.

Also prohibitive are the melodic demands placed upon singers who may be required to sing disjunct linear lines against dissonances in other musical parts—something a violinist or keyboard player can perform more easily than the singer, who first must think the pitch and then place the note before actually producing a sound. The fact that many singers begin learning their instruments late in high school is frequently overlooked; many instrumentalists begin playing in elementary school. Male vocalists in particular are at a distinct disadvantage compared to their instrumental peers simply because they may not have a vocal instrument until anywhere between fourteen and eighteen years of age.

My advice to young composers is to keep the listening audience—the public—in mind. It is important to keep in mind that music can have a profound effect on people, arousing complex feelings and emotions. As much as I appreciate the complexities and intricacies of much serialism, for instance, I have yet to feel emotionally fulfilled or moved by any work of Berg's or Webern's.

By the same token some minimalist works of Arvo Pärt, John Tavener, and Philip Glass have had a profound effect on me. I don't think the future of music is to write more "academically" or in a cold style; the future of music lies in the writing of music from the souls and hearts of composers. The general population is mostly musically uneducated but will respond to something emotionally or spiritually touching. Audiences do not respond as well to music that is stark, irrelevant, or meaningless. Composers should be true to the listening audience by writing music that is touching and meaningful without cheapening or diluting the musical or textual content. The general public is, after all, one of the most important factors in the entire process.

J. Comprehensive List of Works for Choir

All pieces are published by Santa Barbara Music Publishing unless otherwise noted.

Mixed Voices:

A Blessing, SATB, piano and flute (SBMP 504)

Ave Verum Corpus, SATB, a cappella (SBMP 462)

Cantate Domino, Benedicamus Domino, SATB, one piano/four hands, trumpet, Alliance Music Publications (AMP 0517)

Fill My Life with Spring, SATB, piano (SBMP 680)

He Wishes for the Cloths of Heaven, SATB, piano and flute (SBMP 563)

Hymn to St. Cecilia, SATB, a cappella (SBMP 436)

I Will Come to You, SATB, a cappella (SBMP 668)

I Will Lift Mine Eyes to the Hills, keyboard (SBMP 667)

In Remembrance, SATB and solo soprano, a cappella (SBMP 538)

O magnum mysterium, SATB, a cappella (SBMP 211)

O nata lux, SATB, a cappella (SBMP 562)

O vos omnes, SSAATTBB, a cappella (SBMP 329)

Prayer of St. Francis of Assisi, SATB, piano, violin or flute (SBMP 296)

Rise up My Love, SATB, flute, keyboard, Colla Voce Music (36-22010)

Salve Regina, SATB, a cappella (SBMP 248)

Set Me as a Seal Upon Your Heart, SATB, keyboard, trombone or French horn (SBMP 210)

Sonnet of the Moon, SATB, piano (SBMP 577)

The Lord Is My Shepherd, keyboard, French horn or trombone (SBMP 250)

The Messenger, SATB, *a cappella* (SBMP 689)

The Moon Is Distant from the Sea, SATB, piano (SBMP 540)

Think on These Things, SATB, keyboard (SBMP 629)

Two Songs of Reflection, SATB, *a cappella*, Alliance Music Publications (AMP 0390)

When You Search For Me, keyboard, flute, Colla Voce Music (36-22007)

Where Dwells the Soul of My Love, SATB, piano, oboe or flute (SBMP 463)

Men's Voices:

Fuji, TTBB, piano (SBMP 636)

O sacrum convivium, TTBB, *a cappella* (SBMP 627)

Prayer of St. Francis of Assisi, TTBB, piano (SBMP 637)

The Lord's Prayer, TTBB, keyboard, flute (SBMP 212)

Weep No More, TTBB, piano (SBMP 490)

Women's Voices:

Ave Maria, SSA, piano and flute (SBMP 222)

I Am Not Yours, SSAA, piano (SBMP 568)

Life's Loveliness, SSA, piano (SBMP 551)

Love's Philosophy, SSA, piano (SBMP 628)

Prayer of St. Francis of Assisi, SSA, piano, violin, or flute (SBMP 401)

She Walks in Beauty, SSAA, piano and oboe (SBMP 435)

Song of Ruth, SSAA, piano (SBMP 539)

The Lord's Prayer, SSA, keyboard and flute (SBMP 224)

Weep No More, SSAA, piano (SBMP 249)

rené
Clausen

A. Biography

R ené Clausen (b. 1953) is known nationally and internationally as a premier conductor and composer. As conductor of the Concordia Choir at Concordia College in Moorhead, Minnesota, since 1986, Clausen has continued the choir's outstanding tradition and furthered its reputation at home and abroad by developing an ensemble sound that blends rich aesthetic expression, tonal refinement, and technical skill, serving as a model for choirs throughout the country.

René Clausen is also a well-known composer and arranger, having written more than fifty commissioned compositions frequently performed worldwide. His compositional style is varied and eclectic, ranging from works appropriate for high school and church choirs to more technically demanding compositions for college and professional choirs.

Clausen is interested in composing for various media; he has written works for the stage, solo voice, and film and video as well as choral-orchestral compositions and arrangements and works for orchestra and wind ensemble. He is commissioned on a regular basis, and some special commissions include *Canticle of Praise*, written for the King's Singers and the Mormon

Tabernacle Choir as well as all of the choral scoring and arrangements for the musical T*E*X*A*S.

Clausen has written commissions at the request of the
American Choral Directors Association on two separate
occasions. In 1994 he composed Crying for a Dream, a three-
movement work based on Native American themes, which
premiered at the North Central Regional ACDA convention in
Rapid City, South Dakota. In 2002 the ACDA invited Clausen
to write the prestigious Raymond W. Brock Memorial
Commission for the 2003 National ACDA Convention in New
York City. Written for chorus, orchestra, and baritone solo, his
composition MEMORIAL was inspired by the tragic events of
September 11, 2001, in New York City and was premiered by the
Concordia College Choir and Orchestra at Lincoln Center on
February 15, 2003.

The compositions of René Clausen have been the subject of
two doctoral dissertations: "The Choral Music of René Clausen"
by Todd Guy (Ball State University, 1997) and "Four Twentieth-
Century Choral Settings of Walt Whitman's Poems by American
Composers" by John F. Warren (University of Miami, 1999).

Clausen is in frequent demand as a guest conductor, guest
composer-in-residence, lecturer, and motivational speaker in the
United States and Europe. In addition to choral conducting,
Clausen has also conducted some well-known literature for choir
and orchestra, including the Brahms Ein deutsches Requiem and
Mozart Requiem and Mass in C Minor at Carnegie Hall.
Additionally, he conducted the New York premiere of four of his
own works: Gloria (in three movements), Whispers of Heavenly
Death with text by Walt Whitman, Communion with text by
George MacDonald, and Hellas: In the Name of Freedom—1821,

commissioned by Mid-America Productions of New York City in celebration of Greek Independence Day, all at Carnegie Hall.

In summer 1998 Clausen held the first René Clausen Choral School held on the campus of Concordia College in Moorhead, Minnesota. More than a reading workshop, the choral school is an intensive, five-day program for choral conductors that focuses on conducting and rehearsal technique, performance practice issues, ensemble skills, and tonal development as well as daily reading sessions of new music. Recent guest faculty members include Dale Warland, Eric Whitacre, Anton Armstrong, André Thomas, Weston Noble, Sigrid Johnson, Z. Randall Stroope, and Rollo Dilworth.

René Clausen has served as the senior editor of Mark Foster Music Company. He also was interim conductor of the National Lutheran Choir of Minneapolis, Minnesota. Clausen is a graduate of St. Olaf College in Northfield, Minnesota, and received his master of music and doctor of musical arts degrees in choral conducting from the University of Illinois–Urbana-Champaign. To learn more about René Clausen, his music, and activities, visit www.reneclausen.com.

René Clausen is married (1974) to the former Mary Francis (Frankie) Dimick. Together they have three children, Joshua (b. 1981), Kate (b. 1984), and Rachel (b. 1990). The family resides in Moorhead, Minnesota.

***

I have been involved—or shall I say preoccupied—with music for most of my life, beginning with a summer band program in the summer after sixth grade. I started on saxophone but quickly began to play other instruments, checking them out from the public school and learning the fingerings for each from the old Rubank method books. Although I sang in choir throughout my school years, my primary interest was instrumental music.

I heard the St. Olaf Choir perform under Kenneth Jennings when I was a junior in high school, which prompted my growing interest in choral music. I attended St. Olaf but played in the orchestra and band as a freshman, although I also sang in the Chapel Choir. However, by the time I got into the St. Olaf Choir junior year, my primary interest was in choral music. I have been grateful, however, for my wide instrumental background because I feel comfortable in front of an orchestra and in writing and scoring for orchestra and wind ensemble.

I don't remember consciously choosing a career in music, although I was always drawn to music. I think music became a passion sometime in early high school, which is when I began composing and arranging instrumental music. I did an arrangement of a popular 1960s Burt Bacharach tune titled "This Guy's in Love with You" for stage band. I will always remember the thrill of hearing that arrangement performed for the first time.

When I was a senior in high school, three of my friends wanted to play a piece for the small ensemble music contest, but the instrumentation of their trio—bassoon, French horn, and bass clarinet—was a bit of a problem. I didn't know of any music written for that particular combination of instruments, so I wrote a set of three Baroque variations for bassoon, horn, and bass clarinet on "Light My Fire" by The Doors. They wound up going to state solo and ensemble contest and received a "one" rating.

I began arranging and then composing for choirs while I was in undergraduate school at St. Olaf College. I wrote and arranged for my choirs when I started teaching high school and junior high choirs, which gave me immediate feedback about my

28

work. I wrote music for several groups, including the seventh and eighth grade mixed choirs with the typical cambiata ranges for boys at this age, at various stages of voice change. I also arranged music for the ninth grade mixed choir and a concert choir of upperclassmen. I did not publish any of that material.

For many years, I declined to call myself a "real composer," largely because of my lack of formal training. I have never studied composition, having taken only the required theory courses at the undergraduate level. I have, however, studied the music of many composers and their styles and continue to do so. I learn by study and absorption of what other composers have done.

B. The Creative Process

I have a somewhat difficult time with the word "inspiration" as it applies to the art of composition, as composition largely involves making choices about style, melodic and harmonic vocabulary, difficulty level, etc. Having said that, I often find inspiration in a beautiful text, which generates compositional ideas.

Choosing the text is primary. I have to be able to choose a text I can respond to in a creative manner, or I find composition nearly impossible. This is the reason I do not write commissioned compositions to a prescribed or pre-chosen text.

I then proceed to study the text, both in terms of its organization and content and begin asking myself questions: 1) What kinds of musical ideas does the text suggest? 2) What is to be the scope of the piece? 3) Will there be a primary emphasis on one or two elements (melody, harmony, rhythm, etc.)? Then I start fleshing out the piece by writing and developing thematic material. I compose mostly at the piano, initially using paper and pencil, except when I'm writing full orchestrations, in which case I orchestrate directly into the computer.

I'm sometimes asked when I know a piece is done and what tells me to stop writing a piece. This process is simply creative and intuitive, and it is finished when it is finished. I don't mean to be glib—I simply don't have a better answer.

Oftentimes deadlines have created the compositional regimen for me; I have not been very consistent in terms of a regular composition time. Being a full-time choral director is quite time consuming, and I have tended to write during my down time in between teaching and conducting commitments.

C. The Relationship Between Text and Music

I always begin with the text because it might suggest a certain melodic shape. I also decide whether the piece will be unaccompanied or accompanied before I begin, as this often affects my compositional approach. I think accompanied and unaccompanied pieces are conceptually quite different. An accompanied piece needs to be thought of as an organic process, combining the voices and accompaniment, which is not the case in unaccompanied writing.

As I said earlier, I need to be able to choose a text I know I will respond to; I simply don't choose texts that don't evoke a strong response. I have chosen many texts from the Bible—in particular the psalms and other sacred writings. I also find inspiration in the poetry of Walt Whitman and Sara Teasdale, plus a number of modern poets.

D. Views from the Composer to the Conductor Pertaining to Score Study and Preparation

The style of any particular piece primarily generates from two considerations: 1) what the textual content and form might suggest and 2) the intended level of technical difficulty.

If there is a "Clausen" style, I hope it is not too well-defined as I feel that I am still growing, learning, and experimenting as a composer. I'm sure that an overview of my works, like the works of any composer, might reveal certain tendencies or patterns, or pieces that represent a kind of growth. However, I (like most composers) don't spend much time analyzing those tendencies.

As a conductor, I have always tried to seek out the composer's intent. Depending upon when the piece was written, this may include study of proper performance practice—features or conventions of performance assumed by the composer. Conductors who don't do enough score or stylistic study frequently use "license for personal interpretation" as an excuse for an inauthentic performance.

E. The Relationship Between the Composer and the Commissioning Party

I write some pieces with my college choir in mind—both in terms of sound and technical ability. When writing a commissioned piece, I have to keep in mind the age level and technical facility of the ensemble, which can and should be limiting factors.

Writing commissioned music is a double-edged sword. Composing with technical limiting factors in mind (compositions for church choir, high school choir, etc.) is a good discipline for any composer. However, these restraints can also limit a composer's growth in technique. For this reason, I try to keep a balance between composing commissioned music and music that I write free from technical limitations.

I seldom rewrite a piece of music after it has been premiered in front of an audience, although this has happened on occasion. As I have become more experienced I "hear the sound" I intend more accurately and want to portray that in every composition.

F. Views on the Teaching of Composition and How to Mentor the Young Composer

My advice is this: Know the choral instrument to the best of your ability by participating in a choir, preferably a good one. Study every voice type, and be a voice student. The best choral composers know vocal technique and the nuances of the voice. Study the music and compositional techniques of other composers. Get as much feedback as possible about your writing from those who conduct or sing it, and have a thorough understanding of piano technique.

I would not be very good at describing a model curriculum for developing choral composers, because my own background was not focused specifically on composing. I believe a composition curriculum and teacher can only do so much; composers generally teach composition to themselves by study and absorption.

If a certain piece proves to be particularly successful, avoid the temptation to rewrite that piece over and over. Remain open to growth, experimentation, and maturation in your compositional style.

G. Individuals Who Were Especially Influential in My Development and Career

My wife and family are constant sources of support and inspiration.

Kenneth Jennings and Robert Scholz were my primary choral conductors and conducting teachers at the undergraduate level and thus were the first models and mentors who contributed to my development as a choral conductor.

The pieces of Leonard Bernstein and Stephen Sondheim have held particular interest for me compositionally. They both have a wonderful gift of lyricism, poignant expression, and originality without ever straying too far from what is "listenable" for most audiences. For the most part, their compositional efforts have not been cutting edge, new, or experimental but rather have been direct with a strong sense of emotional connection to their listeners. I admire these qualities.

I have also been influenced by my students throughout the years as well as the ACDA and my professional choral and compositional colleagues.

H. Ten Works All Choral Conductors at All Levels Should Study

1. The high Renaissance style of Giovanni Pierluigi da Palestrina and his contemporaries
2. The Motets and Passions of J. S. Bach
3. The American Black Spiritual and its changing style
4. The music of Benjamin Britten
5. The music of Ralph Vaughan Williams
6. The music of Aaron Copland
7. The music of Charles Ives

8. The music of Europeans Arvo Pärt, Henryk Gorecki, and John Tavener
9. The music of the best contemporary Americans
10. World (ethnic) music

The works listed above represent the apex of several types of compositional styles and techniques, music that is worthy of study.

I. The Future of Choral Music

In general, the quality of church music has declined, although many strong individual church music programs still remain. Choral music at the college and university level has flourished, although that may not always be the case if funding for elementary and high school arts programs is cut, as is currently happening in many areas of the country.

There has been a rise of interest in community choirs and semi-professional choirs in most regions of the country. This may be due to the fact that many college singers, upon graduating, are finding fewer quality choirs in the churches, so the community groups have taken their place.

In the area of choral composition, it seems to me that there is a general trend toward writing slower, introspective, and emotional music with an emphasis on thicker textures and vocal timbres. I see less emphasis on complexity at all levels.

Perhaps there is a parallel to this in our society. As technology and the pace of our lives become more complex, perhaps we psychologically desire simpler, more direct musical communication.

Second, the influence of many types of ethnic and world music is being felt in contemporary choral composition. As a result of the ever-expanding capabilities of modern communication technologies that continually make the world smaller, together with a growing realization among many peoples and nations that we are indeed a world community, ethnic folk music and performance traditions are increasingly finding their way into mainstream choral music performance. It is no surprise, then, that these influences are also being seen in choral composition.

J. Comprehensive List of Works for Choir
Mixed Voices:

A Jubilant Song, SATB, *a cappella*, Shawnee Press, MF3048

A New Creation, SATB, SATB soli, orchestra, Shawnee Press, MF2047

All that Hath Life and Breath, Praise Ye the Lord, SATB, soprano solo,
    a cappella, Shawnee Press, MF0223

All This Night, SATB, orchestra, Shawnee Press, MF0587

Alleluia, SATB, *a cappella*, Santa Barbara Music Publishing, SBMP557

At the Name of Jesus, SATB, organ and brass, Shawnee Press, MF2052

Ave Maria, SATB, *a cappella*, Shawnee Press, MF2129

Black Is the Color of My True Love's Hair, SATB, clarinet, Walton Music,
    HL08501551

Bless the Lord, O My Soul, SATB, organ, full orchestration available,
    Shawnee Press, MF2125

Canticle of Praise, SATB/SATB, Santa Barbara Music Publishing,
    SBMP 655

Clap Your Hands, SATB, Shawnee Press, MF2013

Cold December Flies Away, SATB, two flutes, finger cymbals, Shawnee
    Press, MF0543

Come Let Us Sing to the Lord, SATB and brass, organ, Shawnee Press,
    MF2150

Communion, SATB divisi, harp, French horn, organ, Shawnee Press,
    MF2075

Crying for a Dream, three SATB choirs and children's choir, flute,
    Shawnee Press, MF0476

Deep River, SATB, *a cappella*, Shawnee Press, MF2064

Gloria, SATB, brass, Shawnee Press, MF2122

Hosanna, SATB, *a cappella*, Shawnee Press, MF2020

Hymn of Praise, SATB, organ, Shawnee Press, MF0246

I Lift Mine Eyes unto the Hills, SATB, organ, full orchestration available, Shawnee Press, MF2120

I Thank You God, SATB divisi, *a cappella*, Shawnee Press, MF3080

In Pace, SSAATTBB, *a cappella*, Shawnee Press, MF2126

In the Bleak Midwinter, SATB, *a cappella*, Santa Barbara Music

Jabberwocky, SATB, piano, Santa Barbara Music Publishing, SBMP528

Kyrie (from *MEMORIAL*), SATB, organ, Shawnee Press, MF2196

La Lumiere, SATB divisi, *a cappella*, Shawnee Press, MF3072

Laudate, SATB, *a cappella*, Shawnee Press, MF2180

Let All the World in Every Corner Sing, SATB, organ, full orchestration available, Shawnee Press

Magnificat, SSAATTBB, *a cappella*, Shawnee Press, MF0421

MEMORIAL, SATB, baritone solo and full orchestra, Roger Dean Publishing Company, 45/1133R

My God, How Wonderful Thou Art, SATB divisi, *a cappella*, Augsburg-Fortress Publishing

Nunc Dimitis, SATB, keyboard or full orchestra, Augsburg-Fortress Publishing

O Holy Night, SATB, piano or full orchestra, Shawnee Press, MF2195

O Vos Omnes, SATB double choir, soprano solo, *a cappella*, Shawnee Press, MF0420

Oh My Luve's Like a Red, Red Rose, SATB, violin, cello, and piano, Shawnee Press, MF3065

On the Mountain Top Blows the Wind Mild, SATB, *a cappella*, Shawnee Press

Peace I Leave with You, SATB, *a cappella*, Shawnee Press, MF2079

Plenty Good Room, SATB divisi, *a cappella*, Santa Barbara Music Publishing, SBMP536

Psalm 100, SATB, two pianos, Shawnee Press, MF5002

Psalm 108, SATB, organ, Santa Barbara Music Publishing, SBMP543

Psalm 148, SATB, organ, Shawnee Press, MF0267

Psalm 150, SATB divisi, organ or full orchestration, Shawnee Press, MF2128

Psalm 23, SATB, organ, Shawnee Press, MF2165

Psalm 67, SATB divisi, *a cappella*, Shawnee Press, MF2110

Seek the Lord, SATB divisi, *a cappella*, Shawnee Press, MF2009

Set Me as a Seal (from A *New Creation*), SATB, *a cappella*, Shawnee Press, MF2047

Sigh No More Ladies, SATB, piano, Shawnee Press, MF3044

Simple Gifts, SATB divisi, *a cappella*, Shawnee Press, MF0292

Softly and Tenderly, SATB, *a cappella*, Shawnee Press, MF2151

Song at Dusk, SATB divisi, *a cappella*, Santa Barbara Music Publishing, SBMP505

Tant que je vive, SATB, piano, Santa Barbara Music Publishing, SBMP621

Thank the Lord, SATB, *a cappella*, Shawnee Press, MF163

The Early Bird, SATB divisi, soprano solo, *a cappella*, Santa Barbara Music Publishing, SBMP645

The Lord's Prayer, SATB, *a cappella*, Shawnee Press, MF2108

The Prayer of St. Francis, SATB, *a cappella*, Shawnee Press, MF2087

The Road Not Taken, SATB, piano, Shawnee Press, MF3059

The Salutation of the Dawn, SATB, piano, Shawnee Press

The Stairs Behind the Sky, SATB, *a cappella*, Santa Barbara Music Publishing, SBMP584

The Water Is Wide, SATB , clarinet, French horn, cello, piano, Shawnee Press, MF3038

There Is a Balm in Gilead, SATB divisi, soprano and/or tenor solo, *a cappella*, Santa Barbara Music Publishing, SBMP611

There Is No Rose, SATB divisi, harp, cello, optional piano, Santa Barbara Music Publishing, SBMP579

Three Whitman Settings, SATB divisi, Shawnee Press, MF3042

Through Our Beating Hearts Reminds Us, SATB, organ, Shawnee Press, MF2148

To Everything There Is a Season, SATB, oboe, Shawnee Press, MF2181

Tonight, Eternity Alone, SATB divisi, *a cappella*, Shawnee Press, MF3034

Two Songs of Parting (1. There Is an Old Belief, 2. An Irish Blessing), SATB, *a cappella*, Shawnee Press, MF3060

Ubi caritas, SATB divisi, *a cappella*, Shawnee Press, MF2156

Veni, SATB divisi, soprano solo, *a cappella*, Shawnee Press, MF5003

Whispers of Heavenly Death, SSAATTBB and orchestra, Shawnee Press, MF3047

Women's Choir:

All That Hath Life and Breath, Praise Ye the Lord, SSAA, soprano solo, *a cappella*, Shawnee Press, MF0926

Barter, SSA, piano, Santa Barbara Music Publishing, SBMP527

I Am Jesus' Little Lamb, SA, flute and piano, Shawnee Press, MFYS0301

Laudamus Te, SSA and Orff instruments, Shawnee Press, MF0920

Morning Has Broken, SSA, piano, Shawnee Press, MF0935

Psalm 100, SSA, two pianos and instruments, Shawnee Press, MF0917

Set Me as a Seal (from *A New Creation*), SSAA, Shawnee Press, MF0925

The Sun Has Climbed the Hill, SSA, piano, Shawnee Press, MF0975

Turn Around, SSA, piano, Santa Barbara Music Publishing, SBMP542

Men's Choir:

A Jubilant Song, TTBB, *a cappella*, Shawnee Press, MF1073

All that Hath Life and Breath, Praise Ye the Lord, TTBB, *a cappella*, Shawnee Press, MF1023

Set Me as a Seal (from *A New Creation*), TTBB, *a cappella*, Shawnee Press, MF1027

chapter **3**

libby
Larsen

A. Biography

L ibby Larsen, born December
24, 1950, in Wilmington,
Delaware, has created a catalogue
of more than two hundred works
spanning virtually every genre,
from intimate vocal and chamber
music to massive orchestral and
choral scores and seventeen operas. Her music has been praised
for its dynamic, deeply inspired, and vigorous contemporary
American spirit. Major artists, ensembles, and orchestras around
the world seek to commission and premiere Libby Larsen's
compositions, which has helped her works find a permanent
place in the concert repertoire.

Libby Larsen has received numerous awards and accolades,
including a 1994 Grammy for producing the CD *The Art of Arlene
Augér*, an acclaimed recording that features Larsen's *Sonnets from
the Portuguese*. Her opera *Frankenstein, The Modern Prometheus* was
selected as one of the eight best classical music events of 1990 by
USA Today. The first woman to serve as a resident composer with
a major orchestra, she has held residencies with the California
Institute of the Arts, the Arnold Schoenberg Institute, the
Philadelphia School of the Arts, the Cincinnati Conservatory,
Peabody Conservatory of Music, the Minnesota Orchestra, and the

Colorado Symphony. Larsen's many commissions and recordings are testaments to her fruitful collaborations with world-renowned artists such as The King's Singers, Benita Valente, and Frederica von Stade, among others. Her works are widely recorded on labels such as Angel/EMI, Nonesuch, Decca, and Koch International.

Libby Larsen is a vigorous, articulate champion of contemporary music and musicians. She held the Harissios Papamarkou Chair in Education at the Library of Congress 2003–04 and was a recipient of the Eugene McDermott Award in the Arts from the Massachusetts Institute of Technology as well as a Lifetime Achievement Award from the American Academy of Arts and Letters. In 1973 she cofounded the Minnesota Composers Forum, now the American Composers Forum, one of the nation's most active and valuable advocate organizations for composers. Consistently sought after as a leader in the generation of millennium thinkers, those whose art and experience bridge the span between the 1900s and 2000s, Libby Larsen's music and ideas have refreshed the composer's role in the concert music tradition.

***

I grew up in the Midwest and went to Christ the King School in Minneapolis, Minnesota. During my first eight years of school, I sang only Gregorian Chant. We were taught to read music in the same way we were taught to read English, and we sang all the time. That experience caused me think of music as an essential logic rather than as a performance art. Because of this approach, I have no hierarchical feeling about orchestral and choral music, reggae, hip hop, rock and roll, and so on. To my ear, all these musical styles are systems of pitch and rhythm logically evolved by cultures to reflect their sense and definition of music.

Although everyone participated in the Gregorian chant masses, weddings, and funerals and the ritualistic music of the service, the school children made up the choir for all of these events. I first learned to express myself through music by vocalizing. We sang everything in Latin in a style that was modal and without meter. Before the influence of the Second Vatican Council we literally had to learn hundreds of chants.

No one in my family is a practicing professional musician, but music was always a part of our lives. My dad was an amateur clarinet player in the community band; my mother took piano lessons as a child, but I've never heard her play. I remember standing at the piano as a child while my sister was playing. I was about three years old, so my eyes were level with the keyboard. As I was holding onto the piano (and maybe even gnawing on it a little), I remember feeling the vibrations and knowing that she was somehow making that sound with her fingers. I couldn't wait for my turn.

As soon as my sister finished practicing, I climbed up onto the piano stool and composed a piece of music. It was just a series of clusters I came up with, ordered, and restructured, but when I had played my piece through I hopped down and found my mother in the kitchen to see what she thought of my piece.

My seventh grade teacher at Christ the King School, Sister Timothea, taught us our subjects through the various arts. She somehow recognized my desire to write music and asked me to compose a class song and notate it on the board. It was so rewarding to draw the staves, write out my tune, put down my own words, and have it performed—the class sang it every day.

I went to Southwest High School in Minneapolis, where I sang in the choir, took piano lessons, and sang in a rock band.

High school choir was my first experience singing part music and working for a conductor even though I had received wonderful vocal training while singing chant. Chant, as you know is unison singing and has no conductor. I was placed in the second soprano section because I could read music. During my junior year, I decided to compose for the choir. I hadn't really thought of writing part music before, and I was curious about how to translate meters and key signatures into choral music.

To compose for the choir, I needed to develop an understanding of the way the voices worked in relation to the fixed pitch of the piano. When I first sang in an SATB choir, singing with a piano seemed quite out of tune to me; I had to learn how to sing in twelve-tone equal temperament. After that initial adjustment, I was able to compose my piece. I continued composing choral music because I enjoy expressing music through words and through a communal vocal experience.

Between my junior and senior years in high school, I attended a summer program at the Twin Cities Institute for Talented Youth. That summer I became convinced that I wanted to spend my life writing music. I had always composed music—it was just something I did for fun—but that summer when we studied Paul Hindemith, music theory, the spiral of fifths, and the physics of tuning, exposure to the natural tuning system was my beautiful "aha" moment. I was so fascinated by tuning systems, I decided I wanted to spend my life living in sound.

To prepare for my college audition, a professor friend of mine counseled me to sing a piece that showed off my voice to its best advantage. I confess that I felt unmercifully awkward singing in a dress and high heels with proper concert demeanor but took a breath and sang my song—"Georgie Girl." The look of shock, amusement, and disdain on the faces of the audition committee told me I was doing something horribly wrong.

By the time I graduated from high school, I had an enormous repertoire, including the chant I had studied, piano repertoire, rock and roll, Broadway and boogie, Dixieland, and the television music now heard on Nick at Night. I quickly realized the many styles and genres I had learned were irrelevant to the classical study of music. As a result, I am completely dedicated to the idea that we need to teach students "where they are" from the repertoire of their current musical passion in order to teach them about music itself. Put music at the center of their constellation, and build the world of music around them, from the passion for music itself out to the parameters of music and the various repertoires that inform these parameters.

Sometime during my sophomore year at the University of Minnesota, I began to wonder if I could earn a living writing music. I had been studying voice but decided that I was more of a composer than a singer, and I set out to understand what a professional composer does and how I might become one.

My voice teacher at the University of Minnesota, Lois Wittich, gave me an enormous gift during my sophomore year. She suggested that I write my own songs for my juries. I chose five poems from the Tempest, set them, sang them, and got an A on my juries. Although I didn't recognize it at the time, the gift and mentorship this great teacher gave me was an act of true generosity. Other singers, including voice faculty, asked me to write songs for them to perform. I did, and it became the defining moment of my career; at that point, I knew I was a composer.

In college, I wanted to learn as much as I could about composing and the instruments that I love. I also wanted to work with performers on every piece I wrote so that my music would come alive for both performers and audiences. My private process of writing music always leads to a collaboration with the performer, but at that point the process is only half complete. The final step is to perform the piece for an audience; only then is the composition fully realized.

I believe that the University of Minnesota completely honored this process. The voice faculty asked composition students to write art songs for them to perform. Guitar professors invited young composers into their studios to show them the intricacies of the guitar. The holistic approach to the compositional process was quite extraordinary because the end game was always a professional performance before a concert audience: quite different from the more typical laboratory performance.

I stayed at the University of Minnesota for all three of my degrees because of the rigorous instruction in counterpoint and orchestration and the willingness to use the twentieth-century techniques available at the time. The philosophy was that to become a great artist, you must learn modern techniques to effectively communicate through your art what it is like to be alive to the community in which you live.

I happen to live in Minneapolis, the "buckle of the belt" of choral singing, and I quickly began to work with such renowned conductors as Phillip Brunell and Dale Warland. The choral community is all in sync with the concept "we write, we perform, and we communicate through music," which seems to be a fairly rare occurrence. I sang in Dale Warland's Festival Chorus when I was twenty-two years old and he was a teacher at Macalester College. When he formed the Warland Singers, I auditioned for him and thought I would make it to the final auditions, but I was completely crestfallen when I didn't make the final cut.

However, this solidified my decision to compose. I thought, if I can't sing for him, then I will write for him.

B. The Creative Process

For all of my compositions, I look for a cultural energy, or *Zeitgeist*, a feeling in the air that manifests itself in tempo, energy, and emotion. I am beginning to feel a swing in the pendulum in the culture at large. It seems to me that, for the past thirty or so years, there has been a guarded inertia and hesitancy among composers to express ourselves emotionally through music. Now, I feel the culture itself is almost ready to "sing." For years the media have pressured us to codify the ways in which we live (brands, named communities, demographic identification, etc.), but this is beginning to erode as our confidence in our differences grows and we feel comfortable living together as different and unified at the same time.

Next, I look for a text that allows me to explore this kind of energy. In choral music, I always look to find the music through the text, so finding a text that strongly expresses itself is always my goal in composing for voice. The most important things when setting a text to music are the musicality of the text and my deep connection to those words. I love poetry. I love prose. I read voraciously. When I discover a text I want to work with, I memorize the text and repeat it over and over, using different tempos and inflections until I find the natural flow of the words, the textures, and colors. The text suggests the meter to me—I sometimes think the text sets itself.

In some instances, for example, in a sonnet, a formal meter is imposed on the text of the poem. I would think that formal structure might inhibit great poets such as Elizabeth Barrett

Browning. The opposite is true, of course. The music in the words themselves has a very different meter than the formal meter of the sonnet. I try to find every possible musical nuance of the text as I begin to develop the form of the piece.

I analyze the text for its verbs, nouns, adverbs, and adjectives. I find that the piece will represent itself first from the verbs, suggesting tempo, character, range, and spacing. The nouns must be set very clearly to musically understand the subject (harmonic context), but the verbs are the active part of the text. The adverbs and adjectives suggest the shape of the music. If I am composing opera, I often eliminate the adverbs and adjectives from the libretto and set them in the orchestral color. When the music itself becomes the adjectives and adverbs, you no longer need to hear these words; you will hear them in the music.

I usually work on several texts at the same time in the way I've just described. During this process, I am conceiving the form of the piece and ideas about whether the text is best set as an *a cappella* work or with instruments. I usually hear about half of those as *a cappella* pieces. If I get a commission that calls for a specific instrumentation, I have an archive of texts to consider.

Then I start to put down pitches and rhythms. This is the "magic" part—after I have digested the text, which takes about five-eighths of the composing process—the music seems to come out fully formed. I am not the type of composer who looks for a melodic fragment and begins to build a piece; the textures and dynamics are there and it is just a matter of getting it out of my head and putting it on paper.

I do approach vocal writing and instrumental writing differently. This is in part due to the physical/acoustical properties of the instruments, in part to the musical training of the performers, and in part to the issues that accompany working with text. I can say though that whether I am working with the voice or another instrument, my approach is the same: I work to bring out the natural idiom of the instrument at hand.

I have an "ideal" regimen for composing that seems to rarely work. I strive to write every day, which usually works. Ideally, I write from 9:00–11:00 in the morning and then do the business part of my music. Then I write from 5:00–7:00 in the evening and sometimes from 9:00–11:00 at night . . . at least that is my post-children regimen. When my daughter was growing up, I had to learn another way to work. I learned to compose everything in my head—whole operas would play themselves out. I would then try to sit down with my music from 9:00 in the morning until she would "invade my brain" sometime after lunch. I had to set aside time to "visit my own brain" because the realities of life meant that I did not have the opportunity to visit my thoughts and music any time I wanted. This made me a better composer.

I work at the piano and have a little table next to the piano. I lie down on the piano bench and spread the music paper out on the bench in front of me. I use my left hand to pick out pitches from time to time to check that what is coming out of my brain matches up with the notes I am putting on the page. I have always used this routine, probably lying across my grade-school desk instead of the piano bench when I was young.

For me composing is finding the balance between the moving and standing stillness of music. It is constantly dealing with music's spontaneous spirit while attempting to control its direction. I have had the opportunity to revisit some of my early works and discover how my perspective on composing has changed. I have been attending retrospective concerts of my music because, amazingly, I am "getting old"! When I hear pieces I wrote in the early 1970s, it shocks me to realize how for thirty years I have been developing certain musical ideas without being aware of it. It must the be "muse" at work. I find I have been using and developing certain intervals, I have been fascinated with downbeat rests, I am moving further away from barlines; in short, I have certain habits or ways my brain works.

The business aspect of my world involves a set routine. I have a full-time assistant because keeping up with correspondence is so crucial. If performers and audience members are going to be part of the composing process, the communication, deadlines, and negotiations are also an important part of my process. After the music comes out of the brain of the composer, everything else is negotiated. I keep tidy and organized business records with archives of rehearsal, performance, perception, reception, and perpetuation of works cataloged in a precise filing system.

C. The Relationship Between Text and Music

Each text I ultimately choose to work with inspires me on an emotional level and speaks to me on a musical level. I have set the poetry and prose of Calamity Jane, May Sarton, Bessie Smith, Elizabeth Barrett Browning, Robert Creeley, nursery rhymes, Brenda Ueland, Clyde Tombaugh, and the Bible, among others. Life is what inspires me, and much of what I set to music deals with being alive in some way. It seems that at the outset of a compositional process that involves words, the composer has to make a choice: Will the composer govern the words or will the words govern the composer? In considering this, the central question of composition (where the music comes from) will be greatly influenced by how the composer responds.

I have answered this question both ways, depending on the specific piece at hand. For instance, in "Jack's Valentine" I set the words, bending them to fit my musical idea. However, in "Canticle of the Sun," the words suggested the music to me. What I find most often is that I collaborate, or perhaps negotiate, between the two points of view while working on a texted composition.

Each poem I work with must be considered on its own terms. Great poetry already has its meticulously crafted music—strong and intact. I feel that I have a serious responsibility to work as diligently as I can to discover the music of the poem (or prose) as the first part of my process. If I do that work well, I move beyond the discovery of poetic device to discover the poem's innate melodic contour, meter (usually polymeter), syntax, counterpoint, and musical form. I find that if I stop my process just after the point of analyzing the poetic device, I am more likely to force my music on the poem. But, if I complete my process of discovery to find the music of the poem itself, I open up to the meaning of the poem in an entirely different way, which results in the poem directing the writing of the innate music.

Some texts feel too powerful to me to set to music, for example, Rainer Maria Rilke's, "put out my eyes and I would see thee yet." "Music, When Soft Voices Die" is a text that I could set seventeen different times and the words would always be stronger than the music. There is a piece of mine, a setting of "Little Notes on a Simple Staff," a poem in which the text is so musical on its own that I produced what I believe in retrospect is a weak setting of a very strong poem.

The music that comes out of the text and manifests itself in pitches, rhythms, and textures should at least be able to partner the strength of the text. For me, the music must be more meaningful to the words than the words are to the music.

D. Views from the Composer to the Conductor Pertaining to Score Study and Preparation

When I conceive a piece, I hear it performed very specifically in my head. I challenge myself to translate this performance into information on the page. I want to get onto the page a language that will elicit what I hear in my head's vision of the piece. Of course, it's not possible to hear a performance of my work that exactly matches my own performance. So, over time, I created a ritual with each piece. I look for that moment when I quietly, privately give ownership over to the conductor and the choir. That results in a kind of "default setting performance" that for me approximates an optimal cooperation between composer and performer.

A rather interesting phenomenon has caused my song set *Today, This Spring* to become a conductor's choice. The tempo plot of the three short pieces when performed together is medium–fast–slow, or an allegro "Today, This Spring," followed by a faster "Ray Charles" groove, and ending with the slow and quiet Dickinson poem "If I Can Stop One Heart from Breaking." I deliberately placed the pieces to be performed in that order, however, several conductors have elected to perform the slow piece in the middle. This changes the emotional impact of the piece immensely. An up-tempo ending changes the whole concept (after grief comes renewal, celebration, and peaceful acceptance).

However, as I noted earlier, I make a deal with myself. Ultimately, the pieces I compose belong to the conductor, the performer, and the audience. I work long and hard on setting both the poetry and the text order. I assume that a conductor will look for meaning within the texts themselves and in the order of the texts. I think of preparing the score for performance as being a treasure hunt. I hope all conductors spend some quiet time thinking about why the composer chose the text, what the composer has done with the text, and what musical decisions have been made to enhance and enlighten the text.

I assume that the choir members study the text before they begin working on the music so they can develop their own ideas about the emotional impact of the text before they launch themselves into the technical problems of the music. Often, study of the text's meaning will shed light on what appears to be a technical problem. For instance, composers only have a meager set of symbols (half, quarter, and sixteenth notes; barlines; rests; meters) to deal with, and the text may not call for the type of precision the notation presents. Musical notation is sometimes inadequate to communicate the music. The choir's journey into the text should be the first step in rehearsing the piece. The choir should know not only what the text means but also how the composer set the meaning of the text.

I wish, as a composer, that we could get rid of barlines in choral music. I'm not convinced we need them as much as we think we do. They suggest counting and precision of beat. While precision of beat is useful in certain choral settings, it often confuses the flow and meaning of the text for the audience. In my own compositions, I find that I change meter quite frequently to allow the words to move more naturally. Conductors need to take care to interpret my pieces with that same sense of textual flow.

E. The Relationship Between the Composer and the Commissioning Party

I wrestle with the double-edged sword of writing music to the specifications of the commission and the perceived "sound" of the choir and writing the ideal piece of music. With very few exceptions, I write a piece to fit the sound I hear in my head. I don't necessarily write a piece to fit the specific sound of a specific choir. I choose a text that will generate music I hope the choir can express within their own range of color and ability.

For example, I am composing a work for handbells, clarinet, and choir. The size of the commissioning choir will determine how I voice the piece. Other than this I will not tailor the piece for specific voices in the group. The commission required performing forces for SATB choir and handbells, but I added clarinet to this piece because it needed it. At this point in the process, I can't exactly tell you why.

As an exception to this practice, consider, for example, the "St. Olaf Sound" with which most people are familiar. It asks the female voices to limit their vibrato and create a very focused and clear tone. It is an abstract choral sound. If I had a text that could best be heard through that sound, then I would contact the organization and describe my idea for the piece, or I would wait for a choir with a similar sound to contact me for a commission.

The sound of the choir needs to fit the text. I would like to challenge everyone in the choral field to think of itself in this way. Rather than develop one sound per choir, I challenge the field to train their choirs to produce many sounds for many different texts and styles. We live in a culture that expresses itself normatively and extremely colorfully through its voice. My wish for choirs is that they embrace a range of texts and a range of choral colors. The choir should be technically trained as a multicolor instrument so that communicating through various styles of music will not be so daunting.

I will occasionally rewrite music after it is premiered as I work out some of the small details. Sometimes I readjust the acoustic I heard in my head, and sometimes I renotate the overlap of phrases. Often during rehearsals for the premiere of a piece, the rehearsal process is open-ended to adjust dynamics and subtleties that should go on the page before it goes to press after the premiere.

F. Views on the Teaching of Composition and How to Mentor the Young Composer

There are three things that I would suggest to the young aspiring composer:

1. Listen to as much music as you can, and, if at all possible, follow along in the score. If you are able, feed the music into a computer and examine it as a waveform map. You will learn a great deal about how the music works this way. If this is not possible, try to imagine the score. Set aside prejudices regarding music, and listen to music of all different genres. Adopt the principle that music is a language and all styles of music are simply an expression of the culture to which they belong. If you want to learn music, you need to set aside your likes and dislikes until you know exactly what you like based purely on musical terms.

2. Keep singing! Sing like crazy in every kind of choir you possibly can to better understand breathing techniques, what it is like to work with different conductors, and experience what it is like to sing an entrance on pitch. Psychologically, it is very difficult to come in on your part if you don't feel secure about the next pitch. If you stop singing, you will forget the nuances of the psychology of singing.

3. Work hard at ear training to hear intervals away from the computer and/or piano, and take rhythmic dictation. Record

your voice in a variety of settings such as speaking on the phone, reading out loud, or singing, and write down what you hear in pitches and rhythms. Transcribe any rhythms you hear from everyday sources such as a car engine, a bird song, a conversation, a tap dance, or a music rehearsal to develop a sense of the difference between the metered flow of time and the natural rhythmic flow of our culture.

Work at your music every day. Talk to musicians and music teachers as often as possible and befriend creative and artistic people in music and also writing, painting, sculpting, photography, filmmaking, etc. Young composers must develop a sense of musical rigor and discipline. The best way to do this is to learn keyboard-generated music theory well enough to skillfully analyze music for its pitch content, harmonic content, and rhythmic content. At the same time, it is important to learn music theory, form, and analysis through the perspective of Bach as only one of several systems of music. Young composers already have their own music; what they need to know is how to apply the discipline of traditional music theory to the new principles and rules of their own musical voices.

The traditional academic core of music theory teaches young composers about the discipline of their craft. This provides students with a sturdy foundation, and those who learn to apply that rigor to their own compositional voices can become great artists. The rules and counterpoint of Bach are not always applicable to contemporary music. Students need a foundation in theory to develop their own instincts and skills so they can compose the music that is unique to them.

G. Individuals Who Were Especially Influential in My Development and Career

My earliest music teachers were the St. Joseph of Carondolet nuns at Christ the King School in Minneapolis, Minnesota. Everyone learned solfege in order to read and sing Gregorian chant and learned to sight read using movable *do*. My first grade teacher, Sister Helen Marie, taught us how to use music as a thinking logic first and a performance activity second. This is at the root of why I am a composer.

My piano teacher, Sister Colette, was extraordinarily diverse in the kinds of pieces she gave me to learn. I played unusual repertoire from the start—Mozart, Bartók, Stravinsky, Japanese music, and boogie—and that variety was very important in introducing me to so many different musical sounds and colors.

William Lydell, choir director at Washburn High School in Minneapolis, was the teacher at the summer institute when we studied Hindemith theory and counterpoint. He was trained as a concert pianist, and he instilled in me his sense of rigor and discipline when I was a junior in high school.

My composition teachers at the University of Minnesota— Dominick Argento, Paul Fetler, and Eric Stokes—were all very influential. Vern Sutton, tenor and director of the Opera Theater while I was at the university, offered to perform my first opera if I chose to write one. So I composed an opera, and he did indeed produce it. I can't begin to tell you how it affected my confidence, Vern saying, "If you do it, I will help." He trusted my instincts. Youth is the best thing going for some of us, because I had no idea at that point in my career that operas were thought to be "hard to compose."

Vern Sutton also introduced me to Garrison Keillor, who used me as a composer for the first national broadcast of "Prairie

Home Companion" in 1977. Garrison frequently interviewed me on his morning show as the Walgreen Composer-in-Residence. Vern also introduced me to Philip Brunelle, who has become a dear friend; he has given me a platform in the form of commissions for all of the stretches I have wanted to make in choral music throughout my life.

I was the Minnesota Orchestra's composer-in-residence, along with Stephen Paulus, working with Neville Mariner from 1983–87. I work consistently with VocalEssence, formerly known as the Plymouth Music Series. I also work with the Warland Singers, the Syracuse Children's Choir, Charles Bruffy and the Kansas City Chorale, and James Dearing and his groups. I met Rick Zielinsky from the University of South Florida, and his Polish-school approach to singing with a huge, vigorous sound seemed to work well with some of my texts, so we have worked together as well.

Kirke Mechem is another influential person in my life. He contacted me one day and said, "I like your music, let's know each other." We share a passion for the art of composing music. Kirke is a wonderful early supporter and continues to be a mentor and friend.

My favorite composers are Mozart, Beethoven, Chuck Berry, and Big MaMa Thornton. When I work with young composers, I habitually ask them what they have programmed in their iPods. I used to ask the same question about their CD collections, and before that what was in their cassette collections to find out how they define themselves through their private listening libraries. Almost always, they program a diverse library with a variety similar to my own eclectic tastes. I try to engage them in a discussion of why these musical examples mean so much to them. Then I talk about the music that "is me" and play some examples of my compositions, along with Mozart and Big MaMa Thornton. I ask them to analyze the music to identify how that diverse music has influenced me, and in turn I offer to help them analyze the music that is important to them.

I do quite a bit of residency and master class work in colleges and conservatories. This is part of my own mentoring process to encourage young composers. I believe in person-to-person mentoring. No matter how much technology we introduce into the world of music, at the end of the day, music is a person-to-person communication, and mentoring person-to-person is the through-line of the mysticism of music. I don't completely know why I compose music. I do know that I have a passion to compose. I do know that I love music and feel as if I am the luckiest person alive. When a student comes to me with the same passion, I want to mentor them so that they can live *in* music. No methodology or technology that can teach this type of communication—only people can.

H. Ten Works All Choral Conductors at All Levels Should Study

1. **Song for Snow** by Florence Price. (SATB and piano, 1930; New York: Carl Fischer, 1942, 1957; text: Elizabeth Coatsworth) Florence Price is, hands down, one of the best African American composers of her day. She has been championed by the Chicago Symphony and many other world-class ensembles.

2. **The Dove Descending Breaks the Air** by Igor Stravinsky. (SATB *a cappella*; text: T. S. Elliot) Impeccable twelve-tone choral writing, this deeply emotional work is difficult to master but completely worth the effort.

3. **Totentanz (Dance of Death)** by Hugo Distler. (*a cappella* chorus and speakers) Inspired by the Totentanz fresco at the St. Mary's Church, Distler's music is elegant, clean, and strikingly modernist in the 1930s–40s definition and haunting.

4. **Trois Chansons** by Claude Debussy. (SATB, 1909) Just a masterpiece everyone should learn!

5. **Warum sollt' ich mich denn grämen, BWV422** by J. S. Bach. A transcendent work, this music epitomizes the union of word and music. To sing the first two chords with full intent is to sing the deepest quest of the human condition.

6. **The Word Became Flesh, Op. 162** by Knut Nystedt. (thirteen-part choir, 2001) Well into his nineties, Norwegian Knut Nystedt is a master twentieth-century choral composer. This work should be part of any conductor's repertoire.

7. **Drei gemischte Chöre** by Clara Schumann. (Nauhaus, Gerd, editor; for unaccompanied SATB chorus) These three lovely, masterful works sit well on the voice. They offer an experience with Clara Schumann's compositional work as well as the opportunity for choir members to learn about one of the most celebrated musicians (pianist, chamber musician, and composer) of the Romantic Period.

8. **Lux aeterna** by Gyorgi Ligeti and any of his choral etudes, but in particular **Etude 9, "Csipp, Csepp."** This etude is a mirror canon—short, precise, and extremely witty. The text *is* an icicle melting. This piece is a great way for the choir to learn a little Hungarian, a little about Ligeti, and a little about canonic writing, enjoying themselves all the while.

9. **Steal Away** by William Dawson. If there is only one spiritual that remains forever in the repertoire, I hope it is this one.

10. **Sing Unto God** by Paul Fetler. A gem of a piece, completely and beautifully composed in post-Hindemith modern tonality, with infectious rhythm.

I. The Future of Choral Music

Our approach to the presentational format of our works of contemplation—whether a book, a dance program, or a choral concert—has changed significantly since the 1950s, and an understanding of this format change may be critical to the vision of the future of choral music.

From the late 1800s until about the mid-1980s, the idea that best suited the culture for programming theatre, dance, and music, was for a number of people to gather at a specified time in a specified place for a predetermined program of the art form. Time and place were agreed upon assumptions in the culture at large. This is what we call concert format.

Since that time, the preference for a set time and place has radically changed. Rather than setting aside a Friday evening to enjoy an artistic work of some kind, our culture has evolved our "art delivery system"; an individual can access the art and the moment of contemplation at any place on the globe and at any time of day. This change is real and here to stay.

Choral music as we know it from Robert Shaw through the mid-1980s flourished in the traditional concert format of place, time, and program determination. Since that time, now that we have an entirely new music delivery system, choral music seems to be in the best position of all of the performing arts to customize its presentation format to meet the changing demands of our culture. For instance, why not rehearse and perform a traditional concert and at the same time digitally record a "dress rehearsal," uploading the selection? In this way:

1. The choir members can access their rehearsal as they are preparing the concert.
2. The audience members can familiarize themselves with pieces.
3. Those who can't come to the concert come as a cyber-audience.
4. Each selection can be linked to further interest sites such as 1) the score, 2) photos, 3) information about the piece, and 4) non-choir members' interdisciplinary work, using the music as their point of departure.

There is a host of exciting new possibilities for revitalizing and reinventing our definition of "the concert." Whether the field takes advantage of this is up to the professionals. There are great advantages to gathering to hear live music in a congregated manner. Those advantages need to be trumpeted rather than simply assumed. Conversely, the opportunities for choral music to expand and evolve with the changing times are numerous. I am, in a healthy Scandinavian way, worried that the field may be complacent in its format and therefore miss its opportunity to establish an even stronger position in the arts.

The traditional concert experience evolved around acoustic sound. The new concert experience evolves around produced sound. We need to expand our knowledge of performance practice techniques in the recording studio and come to grips with the microphone to fully train our students. The repertoire of produced sound is only now forming. The future of musical endeavors that require highly developed musicians and music teachers is burning brightly. Our students must be even better musicians than we are now to deal elegantly and expertly with the two cores of sound, the acoustic core and the produced core. We must apply performance standards and pedagogy to the music that inhabits the lives of the students and the audiences who surround us. These students have passion, skill, and curiosity and come to us for help. They are our future.

We must encourage the next generation to compose the music that is inside of them using the best technique that they can. The goal of composition should not be to write music for a prescribed marketplace; rather, it should be to compose highly inspired, communicative music, using the best of our technical skills to communicate something about what it is like to be alive. If the choice is between composing inspired music and composing for the marketplace, please choose inspiration!

J. Comprehensive List of Works for Choir

(LL) = Libby Larsen; (ECS) = ECS Music; (OUP) = Oxford University Press

Mixed Voices:

A Choral Welcome, SSAATTBB and keyboard or orchestra;
   G. Galina, text; 1994 (LL)

A Creeley Collection, SATB, flute, percussion, piano; five movements;
   Robert Creeley, texts; 1984 (ECS #4138)

A Garden Wall, unison choir, keyboard, Orff instruments, two adults,
   five children with speaking roles, congregational singing
   (ECS #4142)

A Salute to Louis Armstrong, SATB chorus, piano; from the choral
   suite "Seven Ghosts"; 4:00; 1999 (OUP #386228X, instrumental
   parts on rental)

And Sparrows Everywhere, SATB, piano; Keith Gunderson, texts
  (ECS #3106)

By a Departing Light, SATB, *a cappella*; Emily Dickinson, texts; 9:30;
  1999 (LL) movements: Bind Me—I Can Still Sing, In This Short
  Life, By a Departing Light, Adrift! A Little Boat Adrift!

Clair de Lune in Blue, SATB jazz choir, piano; textless; 1986
  (ECS #4249)

Come Before Winter, SATB, baritone solo, orchestra or piano;
  Arthur Mampel, text; 2003 (LL)

Coming Forth into Day (Symphony No. 2) soprano, baritone, SATB,
  full orchestra; various texts; 45:00; 1986 (ECS: study score #4135;
  full score and parts on rental)

Dance Set, SATB, clarinet, cello, percussion, piano; textless; 8:00;
  1980 (ECS #3091)

Eagle Poem (see *Missa Gaia*: Benediction) SATB, four-hand piano; Joy
  Harjo, text; 1992 (ECS #4807)

Eleanor Roosevelt, soprano (2), mezzo-soprano, speaker, SATB chorus,
  clarinet, violoncello, piano, percussion played by chorus; Sally M.
  Gall, text; 1996 (OUP #3861542)

Everyone Sang, SATB, harp, 2 percussion; Sigfried Sassoon, text; 1983
  (ECS #4052)

Falling, SATB chorus, SATB quartet, SAT trio, trumpet, piano,
  percussion; James Dickey, text (LL)

Fanfare and Alleluia, SATB, brass, handbells, chimes, organ; 1995
  (OUP parts: #3860422, chorus: #3860414)

Flee We to Our Lord, SATB *a cappella*; Julian of Norwich, text; 4:00
  (LL)

Here's to an Opening and Upward, SATB, *a cappella*; E. E. Cummings,
  text; 1999 (LL)

How It Thrills Us, SATB, *a cappella*; Rainer Marie Rilke, text; 1990
  (ECS #4669)

I Find My Feet Have Further Goals, SATB unaccompanied;
  Emily Dickinson, text; 3:00; 1997 (OUP #3861526)

Invitation to Music, SATB, string quintet or string orchestra
(or piano); Elizabeth Bishop, text; 5:00; 1995 (OUP: vocal
#3860708, score/parts on rental)

Jesus, Jesus Rest Your Head, three- or two-part chorus, solo voice,
piano; traditional, text; 4:00; 2004 (LL)

Little Notes on a Simple Staff, SATB, piano; Siv Cedering, text
(ECS #4806)

Lord, Before This Fleeting Season, SATB, *a cappella*; Maryann Jindra,
text; 2000 (OUP #3864088)

Love and Friendship, SATB, Emily Bronte, text; 1996 (LL)

Love Songs, SATB, piano; based on love poems by American women
poets Muriel Rukeyser, Jeanne Shepard, Bessie Smith, Willa
Cather, Angelina Weld Grimke; 18:00; 1997 (OUP#386133X)
movements: Looking at Each Other, Clinging, Dirty No Gooder
Blues, Dear Love, At April

May Sky, SATB, *a cappella*; Tokuji Hirai, Neiji Ozawa, Reiko Gomyo,
Suiko Matsushita, text; 5:30; 2002 (OUP #3866226) premiere:
Okubo Mixed Choir, Sixth World Choral Symposium,
Minneapolis, Minnesota

Reasons for Loving the Harmonica, SATB and piano; text by Julie Kane;
1997 (OUP #3866218)

Roll over Beethoven, SATB, piano; 1994 (LL)

Sea Change, SATB *a cappella*; texts by Martha Sherwood and John
O'Donohue; 8:00; 2000 (LL) premiere: Los Angeles Master
Chorale, Paul Salamunovich, conductor

Seven Ghosts, SATB, soprano solo, brass quintet, piano, percussion;
five movements, 23:00; twentieth-century biographical texts;
1995 (OUP: vocal #3860082, full score and parts on rental
OUP/Carl Fischer) movements: Grace and Glory, Jenny Lind to
Harriet Beecher Stowe, Blinking Pluto, Myself with Wings,
United Hot Clubs of America)

She's like a Swallow, SATB, flute, piano, folksong text; 1981
(ECS #3107)

So Blessedly It Sprung, SATB, oboe, viola, harp; twelfth-century
poetry, Old English, Adam of St. Victor; 23:00; 1996
(OUP: vocal #3861291, full score and parts on rental OUP/Carl
Fischer)

Songs of Youth and Pleasure, SATB *a cappella*; four movements,
Renaissance text; 1986 (ECS #4290-4293) movements: Song for
a Dance, Pluck the Fruit and Taste the Pleasure, Kisses, Hey
Nonny No!

Sweet and Sour Nursery Rhymes, SATB, French horn; nursery rhyme
text; 9:00; 1998 (OUP: vocal #386276X , horn #3862778) movements: There Was a Little Girl, Little Boy Blue, Try, Try Again

Ten Times Tallis, SATB, *a cappella*; 1999 (LL) premiere: Plymouth
Music Series, Philip Brunelle, conductor; June 3, 1999

The Settling Years, SATB, woodwind quintet, piano; pioneer texts;
three movements, 11:30; 1988 (ECS #4286, parts on rental)

To a Long Loved Love, SATB, string quartet; Madeline L'Engle, texts;
1999 (LL)

Today, This Spring, movements: She Piped for Us, If I Can Stop One
Heart from Breaking (upper voices and piano, OUP#95.417)

Western Songs, SATB, *a cappella*, American Folksong, text; 2005
(OUP) movements: Buffalo Gals #019-3869381, Green Grow the
Lilacs #019-3869403, The Ol' Chisholm Trail #019-386942X

Women's Voices:

A Young Nun Singing, SAA, *a cappella*; anonymous, Sor Juana Inés de
la Cruz, Idea Vilariño, text; 6:00; 2003 (OUP#386855.5) movements: Now That I'm Young; I Want to Be, Mother; My Parents,
As If Enemies; There's Nobody

Canticle of Mary, SSA, four-hand piano or chamber orchestra;
Magnificat, Gregorian Hymnal, text; 9:00; 1994 (OUP:
piano/vocal #385985.8; full score and parts on rental, OUP/Carl
Fischer)

Canticle of the Sun (choral), SSAAA chorus, finger cymbals, synthesizer, organ; St. Francis of Assisi, text; 11:30; 1987 (ECS #4215)

Day Song, SSA chorus, *a cappella*; N. F. S. Grundtvig/L. L., text; 4:00; 1999 (OUP #3862417)

Eine Kleine Snail Music, SA and contrabass; May Sarton, text; 3:00 (OUP #3864355)

How-to Songs, SSA (children's) chorus; 2000 (LL)

I Just Lightning, SSAA, percussion; Maria Sabina, text; 7:00; 1994 (OUP: vocal #3860449, percussion: #3860457)

Jack's Valentine, SSAA, *a cappella*; Aldeen Humphreys, text; 2:00; 2000 (OUP #3865955)

Of Music, SSAA, four-hand piano; Emily Dickinson, text; 9:00; 2005 (LL)

Refuge, SSAA *a cappella*; Sara Teasdale, text; 5:00; 1988 (ECS #4399)

Ring the Bells, SSA chorus (children), piano; MK Dean, text; 2:00; 1998 (OUP #3861534)

Stepping Westward, SSA, handbells, oboe, marimba; Denise Levertov, text; 1998 (ECS #4400)

The Ballerina and the Clown, SSA chorus and harp; Sally Gall, texts; 2002 (OUP #3866730)

The Witches' Trio, SSAA, *a cappella*; William Shakespeare, text; 4:00; 2000 (OUP #3863952)

The Womanly Song of God, SSSAAA, *a cappella*; Catherine de Vinck, text; 2003 (OUP #3867559)

Today, This Spring, SA, piano; three songs; Emily Dickinson, Charles Wilson, Jan Kimes, texts; 8:00; 1995 (OUP #3860406)

Touch the Air Softly, SSAA, *a cappella*, William Jay Smith, text; 2000 (LL)

Choral with Orchestra:

A Choral Welcome, SSAATTBB and keyboard or orchestra; G. Galina, text; 1994 (LL)

Canticle of Mary, SSA, four-hand piano or chamber orchestra; Magnificat, Gregorian Hymnal, text; 9:00; 1994 (OUP: piano/vocal #3859858; full score and parts on rental, OUP/Carl Fischer)

Come Before Winter, SATB, baritone solo, orchestra or piano; Arthur Mampel, text; 2003 (LL)

Coming Forth into Day (Symphony No. 2), soprano, baritone, SATB, full orchestra; various texts; 45:00; 1986 (ECS: study score #4135; full score and parts on rental)

I It Am: The Schewings of Julian Norwich, soprano, countertenor, baritone, SSAATTBB chorus, orchestra; John Mauropus, Folquet de Marseille, Josephus, Konrad von Wuerzburg, Ratpert of Saint Gall, Theodore of Studite, Mechthild of Magdeburg, Psalms 17, 18, 27, 41, 54, text; 16:45; 2002 (LL)

If I Can Stop One Heart from Breaking, SA, orchestra; Emily Dickinson, texts; 2001 (OUP/Carl Fischer: choral parts #385995-5; vocal, full score, and parts on rental)

In a Winter Garden, soprano, tenor, SATB, chamber orchestra; Patricia Hampl, text; 40:00; 1982 (ECS #0031346504)

Missa Gaia: Mass for the Earth, soprano solo, SATB choir, SSA choir (optional), oboe, strings, four-hand piano; G. M. Hopkins, Bible, Maurice Kenny, Joy Harjo, text; 1992 (ECS #4807, also by rental) movements: I. Introit: Within the Circles of Our Lives, II. Kyrie: Mother, Sister, Blessed, Honored, III. Gloria: Pied Beauty, IV. Credo: Speak to the Earth and It Shall Teach Thee, V. Benediction: Eagle Poem

Praise One, SATB, SATB chorus favori, orchestra; Psalms 146, 147, 148, 150 adapted LL, text; 15:00; 2004 (LL)

Ringeltanze, SATB, handbells, string orchestra; five movements; medieval French, text, translated LL; 15:00; 1983 ECS #4200-4205) movements: Welcome, O Hark, the Bells Glad Song, Beautiful Star, Le Petit Nouveau Ne, At Christmas Be Merry, The Shepherds All Are Waking

Song-Dances to the Light, SA, Orff instruments, full orchestra (or
   piano); 17:00; 1994 (OUP) movements: Processional, Sun
   Song–Dance, Wind Song–Dance, Moon Song–Dance, Star
   Song–Dance, Song–Dance of Myself
The Nothing That Is, SATB, baritone solo, three speaking voices,
   orchestra; LL adapted, text; 36:00; 2004 (LL)
Three Summer Scenes, SATB, optional youth chorus, full orchestra;
   texts by William Carlos Williams, Lloyd Frankenburg and
   Maurice Lindsay 1988 (ECS #4366-4368) movements: Primrose,
   The Night of the Full Moon, Picking Apples

Men's Voices:

A *Lover's Journey*, six-voice male *a cappella* group; text by James Joyce,
   William Shakespeare, Goliard poets; 2000 (LL) premiere:
   The Kings Singers; movements: In the Still Garden; St.
   Valentine's Day; Will You, Nill You; Shall I Compare Thee
   to a Summer's Day?
Clair de Lune, TTBB, tenor solo; Paul Verlaine, text; 1985
   (ECS #4197)
Deck the Halls, TTBB, five soloists, piano, handbells; 1992 (LL)
Now I Become Myself, soprano solo, TTBB *a cappella*, May Sarton,
   text; 1992 (ECS)
Welcome Yule, TTBB and strings; 1984 (ECS #4788)

Anthems:

All Shall Be Well, SA choir, soprano, soprano recorder, triangle,
   keyboard (LL)
Alleluia, SATB *a cappella*, 1:00; 1992 (ECS #4829)
Double Joy, SSAATTBB, handbells, organ; Michael Thwaites
   (adapted), text; 4:00; 1982 (ECS #3077)
God as Ribbon of Light, SATB, organ; Sr. Mary Virginia Micka, text;
   5:00; 1993 (ECS #4830)

God So Loved the World, SATB, *a cappella* (OUP #9780193856646)

How Lovely Are Thy Holy Groves (See Missa Gaia: Agnus
  Dei/Sanctus) soprano solo, piano; Chinook Psalter, text; 1992
  (ECS #4807)

I Am a Little Church, SATB, organ; E. E. Cummings, text; 4:00; 1991
  (OUP #9780193868885)

I Arise Today, SATB, organ; St. Patrick's Breastplate (seventh century,
  text; 5:00; 1995 (ECS #4607)

I Lift up My Eyes to the Hills, SATB, handbells, organ; 2007 (LL)

I Love the Lord, SATB, organ; Nathan Everett, text; 4:00
  (ECS #3079)

I Will Sing and Raise a Psalm, SATB, organ; St. Francis of Assisi, text;
  5:00; 1995 (OUP #3860430)

Is God, Our Endless Day, SATB, *a cappella*; Julian of Nowich, text;
  3:00; 1999 (OUP #386409.6)

Mother, Sister, Blessed, Holy (see Missa Gaia: Kyrie) SATB, four-hand
  piano, Gerald Manley Hopkins, text; 1992 (ECS)

Peace, Perfect Peace, SATB, *a cappella*; Isaiah 26:3, Edward
  Bickersteth, text; 2:00; 1985 (ECS #3134)

Pied Beauty (Glory Be to God) (see *Missa Gaia*: Gloria) SATB,
  four-hand piano; Gerald Manley Hopkins, text; 1992
  (ECS #4807)

Psalm 121, SSSAAA *a cappella*, text; Psalm 121, Patricia Hennings
  and John Muir, adapted by LL; 2000 (OUP #0-19-386364-2)

We Celebrate, SATB, piano (organ); John Cummins, text; 3:00; 1985
  (ECS #3080)

Who Cannot Weep, Come Learn of Me, mezzo-soprano, tenor, SSA;
  text from MS 09.38 Trinity College, Cambridge; 6:00; 1985
  (ECS #2854)

morten
Lauridsen

A. Biography

Morten Lauridsen, composer-in-residence of the Los Angeles Master Chorale from 1994–2001 and professor of composition at the University of Southern California Thornton School of Music for more than thirty years, occupies a permanent place in the standard vocal repertoire of the twentieth century. His seven vocal cycles—*Les Chansons des Roses* (Rilke), *Mid-Winter Songs* (Graves), *Cuatro Canciones* (Lorca), *A Winter Come* (Moss), *Madrigali: Six "FireSongs" on Renaissance Italian Poems*, *Nocturnes*, and *Lux aeterna*—and his series of sacred *a cappella* motets ("O magnum mysterium," "Ave Maria," "O nata lux," "Ubi caritas et amor," and "Ave dulcissima Maria") are featured regularly in concerts by distinguished ensembles throughout the world. "O magnum mysterium," "Dirait-on" (from *Les Chansons des Roses*) and "O nata lux" (from *Lux aeterna*) have become the all-time best-selling choral octavos distributed by Theodore Presser, which has been in business since 1783.

In speaking of Lauridsen's sacred works in his book *Choral Music in the Twentieth Century*, musicologist and conductor Nick Strimple describes Lauridsen as "the only American composer in history who can be called a mystic, [whose] probing, serene work contains an elusive and indefinable ingredient [that] leaves the impression that all the questions have been answered. . . . From 1993 Lauridsen's music rapidly increased in international popularity, and by century's end he had eclipsed Randall Thompson as the most frequently performed American choral composer."

His works have been recorded on more than a hundred CDs, three of which have received Grammy nominations, including *O magnum mysterium* by the New York-based ensemble the Tiffany Consort, led by Nicholas White, and two all-Lauridsen discs, *Lux aeterna* by the Los Angeles Master Chorale conducted by Paul Salamunovich (RCM) and *Polyphony* with the Britten Sinfonia conducted by Stephen Layton (Hyperion). His principal publishers are Peermusic (New York/Hamburg) and Peer's affiliate, Faber Music (London).

A recipient of numerous grants, prizes and commissions, Lauridsen was the Composition Department chairman at the USC Thornton School of Music from 1990–2002 and has held residencies as guest composer/lecturer at more than two dozen universities. In 2005 he was designated an American Choral Master by the National Endowment for the Arts. A native of the Pacific Northwest, Lauridsen now divides his time between Los Angeles and his summer cabin on a remote island off the northern coast of Washington state. Further information regarding Lauridsen may be found at www.mortenlauridsen.com.

***

Music has always been an important, integral part of my life. My mother was a pianist, and I began playing piano at an early age in addition to the trumpet. In high school I sang in the church choir and played piano, trumpet, and flügelhorn in dance bands and combos. If I was not performing music, I was listening to music of all sorts—classical, popular, jazz, and the great composers of Broadway, including Jerome Kern, Richard Rodgers, Cole Porter, and George Gershwin, whom I admire to this day for their great legacy of fabulous songs.

After graduating from high school, I went to Whitman College, a small liberal arts college in eastern Washington state. I did not take any music classes that first year of college, concentrating instead on history and English. At the end of my freshman year, however, I auditioned for the noted pianist David Burge, who was professor of music (piano) at Whitman College. He accepted me as his student for the following school year.

The summer after I graduated from high school I worked as a Forest Service firefighter, and the next summer I became a lookout on a remote tower just south of Mount St. Helens in an area that was closed to the public. I spent ten weeks alone at that post, coming down only once for supplies. It was a unique opportunity to have some very deep introspection, and I realized during this period that I needed to get back into music and explore it seriously as a career possibility.

This led me to return to Whitman College and to take every music class available during my second year there: theory, choir, history, instrumental ensemble, and piano. The limited number of course offerings at Whitman, however, made me consider transferring to the University of Southern California School of Music in Los Angeles. During my campus visit to USC, I met with Halsey Stevens, and that meeting became a turning point in my life. I explained that I was considering a transfer to USC because of its fine reputation and my desire to study a wide variety of topics, including composition. I requested that he allow me to take a composition class. He listened with interest and said, "Let me see your portfolio of compositions."

At that point in my musical career, I had none! He said that they couldn't accept me without a portfolio, but rather than dismiss me at that point he instead asked me to play something for him on piano. I performed from memory the Brahms E-flat Rhapsody. Halsey peppered me with questions about literature and stared at me for a long time. Eventually he said, "Upon reconsideration, I will give you one semester and see how you do." This conditional entrance into the Composition Department gave me the opportunity to study with Ingolf Dahl, Harold Owen, and Robert Linn in addition to Halsey Stevens and led to a career where I later succeeded him as chairman of the Composition Department at the USC Thornton School of Music.

Incidentally, my classmates included Michael Tilson Thomas, Martin Katz, Rose Taylor, and Ralph Grierson, among others who later went on to stellar careers in music. As a student I sang in choirs conducted by James Vail and attended many concerts given by the legendary Charles Hirt. This proved to be an invaluable experience for me as a composer for choral ensembles.

B. The Creative Process and
C. The Relationship Between Text and Music

My great love aside from music is poetry. I minored in poetry during my doctoral studies, and I continue to read it every day. In addition, I love the inherently personal sound of the human voice and have always been enamored by art songs and choral music. For these reasons, the core of my compositional output has involved setting words to music. I am constantly reading poetry as a springboard for my compositional output.

The seven vocal cycles I have written all have different compositional approaches and are set to poetry in a multitude of languages—French, Italian, Latin, and Spanish in addition to English. In each case, the compositions are musically geared to complement the style and content of the texts.

The song cycle on poetry by Federico García Lorca, *Cuatro Canciones* for soprano, cello, clarinet, and piano, sets four different texts about night and time. The poetry is unsettling and abstract and, consequently, so is the music, which is atonal, highly colorful and based on small melodic cells. The choral cycle *Madrigali: Six "FireSongs" on Italian Renaissance Poems*, evolves from a single dramatic chord (the "Fire-Chord"), which becomes the impetus for the entire musical cycle, centering on unrequited love. The characteristics of that cycle reflect the procedures and traits of the great madrigalists of the sixteenth century, Carlo Gesualdo and Claudio Monteverdi, with bold harmonic movement, excessive use of dissonance, word painting, and modality.

The *Lux aeterna* was written as a Requiem for my mother. When I received the news that she was dying, I turned to liturgical texts that gave me reassurance and comfort. Using light as the unifying image, I composed a meditative piece referencing procedures and characteristics from sacred music of the high Renaissance, especially the music of Giovanni Pierluigi da Palestrina and Josquin Desprez.

Les Chansons des Roses on Rainer Maria Rilke poems are delicate pieces that reference a more impressionistic palette, and the music evokes soft, hazy memories, aromas, and pastel colors. The *Mid-Winter Songs*, based on poems by Robert Graves and the solo song cycle, *A Winter Come*, are more neoclassical in formal design. Here the music is cool and crisp and has edges and rhythmic vitality. Each of the new *Nocturnes* reflects the nationality and style of the poets—Rainer Maria Rilke, Pablo Neruda, and James Agee.

My teaching schedule allows me to write at home three days a week. I generally work at the piano, as I like to "touch" the sound. I still compose with pencil and score paper and do not use a computer.

I have spent my summers on a remote island off the northern coast of Washington state since I was a young boy. My aunt and uncle had a cabin there, and soon after they sold it in the early 1970s, I was able to buy a remnant of a general store on the island that was built in the early 1900s. The store had been abandoned for at least twenty-five years, but over time I have turned it into a wonderful summer cabin on the western waterfront. It remains very rustic, with no electricity or running water. I finished the "O magnum mysterium" and the *Lux aeterna* in that cabin on an old fifty-dollar piano.

As I sit in that cabin, looking west toward Canada, I am struck by how pristine and unspoiled the island remains without the usual distractions of everyday life. I find unbelievable peace there. Many choristers have commented that this serene feeling has seeped into my music, that some of the pieces I have written have a quietness about them that seems to echo the environment of the island. I spend part of every summer there reading, walking the beaches and woods, and working as a carpenter on my cabin. (Pictures are on my Web site, www.mortenlauridsen.com, including the old piano I use when composing up there.) On the island I feel at one with nature and its unspoiled beauty. My sojourns there are counterpoints to my active professional life. One learns to be very self-reliant on that island, and the islanders have been careful to keep the island preserved in its natural state. It is a magical place.

D. Views from the Composer to the Conductor Pertaining to Score Study and Preparation

Study the poem first. See how the music supports the text, both in overall approach and for the setting of single words. Look for the rhythmic give and take; the use of rubato is important to me, as is tempo. Conductors will find that my pieces tend to settle into a certain tempo that is just right. "Dirait-on," "O magnum mysterium," and the *Lux aeterna* are frequently conducted too slowly and thereby lose the overall feel of the compositional line.

When I put a duration marking on a score, it is important for the conductor to check that timing that against the duration of their rehearsal performance. "O magnum" should not be seven or eight minutes long! When people send me a recording of their performance of my music, one of the first things I look at is the timing. If the timing is way off, I don't even listen to the music because it means the conductor has not followed the tempo and duration that I have suggested. While there is a certain amount of leeway for interpretation, if the tempo is way off the mark, it ruins the piece for me.

The two lines of text in "O magnum mysterium" have inspired composers for centuries. The first concerns the birth of Christ, and the second focuses on the Virgin Mary. My goal here was to underscore those words in a piece that was harmonically and melodically direct, as beautiful as possible, and seemingly ageless, that conveyed a profound inner joy—a piece of quiet radiance. The sorrow borne by the Virgin Mary and her special place in the Nativity drama are underscored by a single note, the appoggiatura G-sharp sung by the altos. This is the only note in the entire piece of music that is out of the key. If conductors study the harmonic language in this composition, they will recognize the influence of *fauxbourdon*. Almost all of the chords "float" in first inversion. The root position is saved for the middle "alleluia" section.

I try to give as much indication to the conductor and the performer in the scores of all my works as to what I want in the performance because it is very important to me that these guidelines be followed. During score preparation, it is crucial for the conductor to sing every line of every part in addition to becoming thoroughly familiar with the music and how it relates to the text. Study not only the poetry, but the poet as well. The conductor has a responsibility to learn the text through the life of the poet.

E. The Relationship Between the Composer and the Commissioning Party

My commissioned compositions are shaped by the particular strengths and expertise of both the conductor and ensemble for whom I am writing. The extensive and virtuosic piano part in the *Mid-Winter Songs on Poems by Robert Graves*, for example, was designed for the Thornton Chamber Choir's brilliant accompanist, Mac Wilberg. The pieces I wrote as composer-in-residence of the Los Angeles Master Chorale underscored Paul Salamunovich's expertise in chant and the Latin liturgy. The prominent alto lines in those works featured a section of the Master Chorale I thought was especially wonderful. (I constantly receive letters from altos from all over the world, expressing their appreciation for featuring this often neglected and under-used voice).

The ultimate shape of my "Ave dulcissima Maria," commissioned for the Harvard Men's Glee Club, resulted from extensive conversations with conductor Jameson Marvin. My setting of "Sure on This Shining Night," the third movement of my recent *Nocturnes* (the Brock Commission for the ACDA) kept in mind Gene Brooks's wish that I compose a work that could be sung by a large number of choruses. (The first two movements of that cycle do require more advanced ensembles.) In each of the many commissions I have undertaken, I have worked closely with the commissioning party and wrote to their strengths; however, I always make the final text selection and all other artistic decisions.

F. Views on the Teaching of Composition and How to Mentor the Young Composer

My first piece of advice to young composers aspiring to write choral music is to sing in a choir to find out what works and what doesn't work. As you start to sing your own part, you will get valuable experience on both the technical side of composing and the choral repertoire.

Second, study scores and attend concerts whenever possible. When I was a composition student in my undergraduate days, I would go to sleep each night listening to a stack of records on my turntable to become familiar with the literature.

Third, young composers who are interested in setting texts to music should read poems and build a vast personal poetry library. I look for beautifully crafted poems that have a universal message, or a symbol that allows them to have many interpretations. Fourth, make connections with groups that might be interested in performing your music. Chamber choirs throughout the country are especially interested in new literature, but the choral world is extraordinary, with excellent conductors and ensembles at every level. Be willing to promote yourself. I have a fine publisher that does that for me now, but when the "O magnum mysterium" was first published, I personally went to the Chorus America conference in Seattle and passed out dozens of copies of the score to conductors at that convention. Composers, especially those starting out, should be proactive with their music and not sit back waiting for things to happen.

G. Individuals Who Were Especially Influential in My Development and Career

I studied composition with four very fine teachers: Ingolf Dahl, Halsey Stevens, Robert Linn, and Harold Owen. I was able to repay Halsey Stevens later in life for his confidence in me and for his generosity. He developed a horrendous case of Parkinson's disease in the 1980s and became physically debilitated. He asked me to go to his studio and see if I could find any promising but unfinished compositions and to finish them in his style (this included his Seventh Piano Sonatina, Viola Concerto, *Four Songs of Love and Death*, and "Venite, exultemus"). He also asked me to be the family adviser on musical matters relating to his estate, which I continue to do to this day. Years ago, Halsey saw some promise in a nineteen-year-old kid from Oregon and gave me an opportunity that I have never forgotten.

The composers who have influenced me the most are the ones who knew what to do with musical line: Franz Schubert,

Johannes Brahms, Robert Schumann, J. S. Bach, and Benjamin Britten, to name a few. The elegant lines that these men composed are a source of inspiration to me, as are pieces by the great Broadway composers mentioned earlier.

H. Ten Works All Choral Conductors at All Levels Should Study

1. The choral works of J. S. Bach (all of them).
2. The choral works of Benjamin Britten, especially the *War Requiem* and *Sacred and Profane*.
3. The art songs of Robert Schumann, Franz Schubert, Ned Rorem, Samuel Barber, Aaron Copland, Gabriel Fauré, and Claude Debussy.
4. The choral works of Johannes Brahms, especially his Requiem.
5. The Requiems of W. A. Mozart, Gabriel Fauré, Maurice Duruflé, and Giuseppe Verdi.
6. The Masses of Josquin Desprez and Giovanni Pierluigi da Palestrina.
7. The madrigals of Claudio Monteverdi.
8. The choral works of Igor Stravinsky, especially the Mass, *Symphony of Psalms*, *Canticum sacrum*, and *Requiem Canticles*.
9. The Six Chansons of Paul Hindemith.
10. Contemporary composers Dominick Argento (Te Deum), James Macmillen (*Seven Last Words of Christ* and *Cantos Sagrados*), Arvo Pärt (*Berliner Mass*).

I. The Future of Choral Music

The choral world is thriving. I do a great deal of traveling around the country and abroad listening to performances and working with choirs of all levels. I have witnessed some very fine work being done by public school teachers, college choirs, and professional and semiprofessional choral ensembles, and it all makes me very optimistic about the future of choral music. The tight-knit choral community, to which I have devoted the majority of my creative efforts, has certainly been very gracious to me and my music over the years, for which I am deeply appreciative.

J. Comprehensive List of Works for Choir
Vocal Cycles:

A *Winter Come* (Moss), high voice and piano, Peermusic

Cuatro Canciones (Lorca), high voice, cello, clarinet and piano,
    Peermusic

Les Chansons des Roses (Rilke), chorus *a cappella*
    (piano on "Dirait-on"), Peermusic

Lux aeterna, chorus and orchestra or organ, Peermusic

Madrigali: Six "FireSongs" on Italian Renaissance Poems, for
    chorus *a cappella*, Peermusic

Mid-Winter Songs (Graves), chorus and orchestra, Peermusic; chorus
    and piano, Opus Music Publishers

Nocturnes (Rilke, Neruda, Agee), for chorus and piano, Peermusic

Sacred Motets:

Ave dulcissima Maria, TTBB chorus *a cappella* (with finger cymbals),
    Peermusic

Ave Maria, SATB chorus *a cappella*, Peermusic

O magnum mysterium, SATB or TTBB chorus *a cappella*, or solo voice
   and piano or organ, Peermusic

O nata lux, SATB chorus *a cappella*, Peermusic

Ubi caritas et amor, SATB chorus *a cappella*, Peermusic

Additional Songs:

Be Still, My Soul, Be Still (Housman), high voice, cello, clarinet and
   piano, Peermusic

Chanson éloignée (Distant Song/Rilke), SATB chorus *a cappella*,
   Peermusic

Dirait-on (Rilke), SATB, TTBB or SA chorus, solo voice and piano,
   mixed duet and piano, and high voice and guitar, Peermusic

O magnum mysterium, solo voice and piano, Peermusic

Where Have the Actors Gone, voice and piano, Peermusic

Additional Choral Works:

Four Madrigals on Renaissance Texts (Jonson and Carew),
   chorus, flute, bassoon, violin, cello, and tambourine,
   Opus Music Publishers

I Will Lift up Mine Eyes, chorus *a cappella*, Peermusic

O Come, Let Us Sing unto the Lord, chorus and piano, organ or brass
   quintet, Peermusic

O Love, Be Fed with Apples While You May (Graves), chorus
   and piano, Opus Music Publishers

Psalm 29, chorus and piano or organ, Opus Music Publishers

kirke
Mechem

A. Biography

Born in Wichita, Kansas, in 1925, Kirke Mechem grew up in Topeka in a creative family. His father was a writer of published novels, plays, and poetry and was director of the Kansas State Historical Society. His mother was a concert pianist.

Mechem began studying piano with his mother at an early age but took lessons for only a few years because he was more interested in sports. He won two national journalism contests as a high school student and later worked as a reporter for the Topeka Daily Capital. During World War II he served two and half years in the army, then enrolled at Stanford University "because they had the best tennis teams." Mechem became captain of Stanford's tennis team, and during the summers he won several state championships as a touring player. Music was a part of his life, although not formally. He played popular music by ear, and at age seventeen began to teach himself to write what he describes as "stacks of wretched songs."

As a sophomore English major, Mechem took a music harmony course out of curiosity. His teacher, Harold Schmidt, was the new choral conductor and required all members of his classes to sing in the chorus. That first rehearsal changed Mechem's life as he listened, sang, and discovered the beauty and power of choral music. At the end of his junior year he switched his major to music, and the very next year he orchestrated and conducted the student variety show. Professor Schmidt became Mechem's mentor and the most important person in his development as a choral composer and conductor, advising Mechem to study composition at Harvard with Randall Thompson and Walter Piston.

After earning a master's degree at Harvard, Mechem returned to Stanford and worked as assistant choral conductor for three years, composing both choral and instrumental music, teaching harmony, and conducting an opera. Professor Schmidt suggested he spend time in Vienna, which proved to be another life-changing experience; for the first time, he was able to immerse himself in hearing and writing music. Near the end of his first year in Vienna, a telegram came from Harvard offering Mechem a teaching and conducting post, but he turned it down to devote as much time as possible to composition. After three years in Vienna (1956–57 and 1961–63) Mechem returned to the San Francisco Bay Area with his wife and children and settled into the house where he still lives. He became composer-in-residence at the University of San Francisco and has also taught at many other universities as a guest composer and conductor.

In 2005 ASCAP registered performances of Mechem's music in forty-two countries. He has composed more than two hundred and fifty published works in almost every genre and style, including two symphonies premiered by the San Francisco Symphony under Josef Krips, and four operas. One of his best-known works is the comic opera *Tartuffe*, which boasts more than three hundred performances in six countries since its 1980 premiere by the San Francisco Opera. He was guest of honor at the 1990 Tchaikovsky Competition in Moscow. He was invited back in 1991 for an all-Mechem symphonic concert by the USSR Radio-Television Orchestra and again in 1996 for the Russian-language premiere of *Tartuffe* at the St. Petersburg Mussorgsky National Theater. He is looking forward to the premieres of his three new operas in the next few years: *John Brown, The Newport Rivals,* and *Pride and Prejudice.*

Mechem is often called the "dean of American choral composers," which he says is because he's "so old." His choral works have been the subject of seven doctoral dissertations and numerous articles. (Adapted from a biography by Helene Whitson, San Francisco Lyric Chorus; reprinted with permission.)

***

There are two ways to look at the above story. My old high school friends look at it in disbelief. When they knew me, I was into everything *but* music: journalism, drama, sports, comedy, and anything else I could think of to avoid studying. But I am beginning to look at my career as inevitable; with my father a writer and my mother a musician, what could be more natural than their having a son who writes choral music and operas?

Beyond this, I now see that my attitudes and beliefs about music—even my compositions—were shaped by the importance of music in my family. Not that we were the kind of family so many musicians come from, in which each child and parent plays an instrument or sings. My mother was the only musician; from the age of five, the piano had been her passion. She had studied as a pianist in Germany and had been accepted as a pupil of

Theodor Leschetizky before World War I forced her to return to this country.

My father was not musically trained—although as a young man he once sang in a quartet that entertained President Taft. Yet he absolutely loved and understood music. During the Depression it was not easy for the mother of four children, with limited means, to spend much time at the keyboard, but my father had wisely made her promise never to let a day go by without playing the piano for at least fifteen minutes. (How many devoted musicians can stop after such a short time?)

We children loved hearing her play after we were in bed. Chopin was her favorite, but we often heard Bach, Beethoven, Schumann, and even Bartók and Gershwin. My mother was a devout Presbyterian and my father an atheist; the common spiritual force in our family was music. She and my father listened to the Metropolitan Opera broadcasts on Saturdays and the New York Philharmonic on Sundays. My mother played at least one recital or concerto every year, and we all understood that these were important events.

In my adolescence my confusions or griefs were assuaged by putting on a record of Ravel, Rachmaninoff, or Bach. Although I do not share my mother's religious beliefs, the beautiful poetry of the Old Testament and the great music it has inspired through the centuries touch the deepest part of my being. It connects me with my mother, who was a wonderful musician, but it also connects me with my father, who was a fine poet (I have set many of his poems to music) and who loved my mother through music just as all of us children did.

Is it any wonder then that I should regard music as something almost sacred? I do not mean sacred in a religious sense. I mean it in the sense that truth is sacred, kindness is sacred, life is sacred.

They are not to be mocked. While I love to laugh at hypocrisy and love humor almost anywhere I find it, I am overly sensitive to what I perceive as the trivialization or brutalization of music or what was common practice in the twentieth century—deliberately making it unintelligible to most music lovers. This wonderful art has room for endless variety, from lighthearted to tragic, from Western to Eastern and everything in between. I am the first to maintain the right of each person to his or her own taste and recognize that just as we all come from different backgrounds, we all have different ways of listening.

I readily admit that my background often determines what I look for in a new piece of music, whether my own or someone else's. I don't want to find new music "interesting" in a purely intellectual way; I am impatient with novelty for the sake of experimentation and I am too old to be taken in by trends or jargon. Been there, heard that. I want to *love* a piece of music, to be delighted by it, to be moved to tears or laughter or in some way taken out of myself. At the very least I must want to hear the piece again, the sooner the better.

We composers are speaking a very old language, and the new ways in which we speak must be understood by our contemporaries. Otherwise we are simply spinning our wheels, and music becomes just another plaything, a hobby, an elitist way of putting down the uninitiated. I prefer it to be the magnificent source of joy and consolation that it has been for generations and was in my own family.

B. The Creative Process and
C. The Relationship Between Text and Music

I have combined these two subjects because they are inextricably linked in the following article I wrote for the Choral Journal, which expresses my views on both. It was published in the November 2003 issue and is reprinted with permission.

The Text Trap

At the heart of choral music is a paradox. A choral piece shapes and is shaped by its text, but because audiences rarely understand the words, they usually hear and judge the piece as pure music.

This paradox represents a double trap for composers. If we obsess over the text, squeezing disparate musical imagery and emotion out of every line, the listener may hear only disjointed musical episodes. If we pay little attention to the text, focusing on the creation of a satisfying musical form, the result may be a disappointing disconnect between words and music.

Today's composers are more liable to fall into the first trap—obsessing on the text. I hear too many new choral pieces that lack musical organization. I'll return to this shortly with some advice on avoiding the text trap, but first let's consider some historical reasons for the modern ascendancy of words over music.

Choral texts today—in this article I am referring chiefly to shorter works—are often secular poems intended to be sung by secular choruses for concert audiences. In the "golden age" of choral music, the texts were more often sacred, sung by church choirs for church congregations. (English and Italian madrigals of the period were written for private singing, not for audiences.) What are the musical implications of the differences between sacred and secular texts?

Secular poems are more varied and less universally known than sacred texts. They may be about practically anything: love, nature, humor, death, morality, music—you name it. This lively variety invites more attention to the text than does one more Gloria, Kyrie, or psalm setting; the congregation already knows most of those texts. Another obvious reason that text has become more important today is that secular poems are usually sung by and for people who speak the language of the poem. Concertgoers are in general more curious participants than Sunday worshipers; they have paid for a ticket and expect to understand what's going on. (Another paradox: we *know* they won't get all the words, but we still expect them to.)

To be sure, choral composers are still writing sacred music. When gifted composers write new and beautiful settings of well-known texts the results are excellent. They concentrate on the music just because the texts *are* so well known. The results are *not* so excellent when composers repeat the formulas of older periods, or set mawkish new texts to mawkish music. I find it interesting that in the choral field, many of the most popular pieces written in my lifetime have been those with well-known sacred texts, e.g., "Alleluia" (Randall Thompson), "O magnum mysterium" (Morten Lauridsen), "Ave Maria" (Franz Biebl). These works are touching, not because of their text settings, but because their music is beautiful and skillfully constructed. (Remember, Bach and Handel sometimes paid little heed to words; they often used the same glorious music for different texts.)

These sacred pieces show one way to avoid domination by the text. However, they do not interest me as much as today's secular choral music, which I believe offers more of an opportunity precisely because secular poetry *is* varied, full of character, and modern in its sensibilities, whether spiritual or worldly. But how often, after hearing a new setting, have we come away with the impression that the composer simply set the poem one line after another with no overall musical plan? This is not composition; it is a catalog of musical ideas: six melodies in search of a composition.

It is not beside the point to observe here that new operas have the same problem. It often seems that the producer, the director, and the librettist have bullied the composer into abdicating his age-old right to be in charge—to compose an opera with dramatic musical forms. Here, too, we often end up with a parade of ideas that lack any substantial musical satisfaction. Great operas have been written to mediocre texts, but none has been written with mediocre music, no matter how good the libretto. Likewise, no choral piece remains in the repertoire because of the text alone.

We choral composers must also exercise dramatic control over our texts and not allow them to bully us into slavish obedience. True, some short poems are so perfectly constructed that the choral composer should simply set them "as is," perhaps as simple homophonic songs. Even so, the music will not sound as perfect as the poem unless the composer's skill in creating a cohesive, integrated work is as great as the poet's.

Recently I decided to test my belief in the primacy of music in choral composition. I wrote a *Suite for Chorus*, subtitled *Songs without Words*, four pieces that use wordless vowels and consonants in somewhat the same way string music uses various bow strokes and pizzicato (not a new idea). While I took great pains to compose the work specifically for choral singers, I had no text to fall back on for emotional content or formal organization. I had only the devices that composers of instrumental music have (which are considerable): melodic and motivic invention, development, repetition, variation, suspense, climax, contrast, unity, variety—and tried to create a satisfying musical journey. For younger composers, and also for experienced choral composers who may suspect that words have been bullying their music, I heartily recommend this kind of wordless discipline. Please don't misunderstand me. I am not advocating that you try to pour your text into a conventional musical form such as sonata, rondo, or ABA. Although I could give you successful examples of all of these, I could also give you disastrous examples.

My first published choral pieces were written more than a half century ago; I have learned from my own mistakes and from the successes and mistakes of others. I cannot presume to tell anyone how to write a good choral piece, but this is how *not* to write one. Good composers—and there are many of them today—can write fine pieces in countless ways, including, perhaps, by ignoring what I am saying. I am only passing on what I have learned.

If I have spoken of a "text trap," don't think for a minute that I believe the text is unimportant. That is where the choral composer begins and where the choral conductor *ought* to begin. But to write choral works with musical integrity the first task is to understand the several kinds of structures in the poem we are going to set, especially the inner, psychological structure on which we will build the musical form. Since the wrong poem may doom us right from the start, the real first task is to *choose* the poem. I sometimes look at several hundred before finding the right one. Whenever I find a promising poem I put it into a file where later it may turn out to be just what I want. (E. A. Robinson's poem "Richard Cory" had been in my file forty years before I found an appropriate place for it last year in the cycle *An American Trio*.)

How do you tell a good poem for choral music from a bad one? First, you have to love it. Poems and music live in the emotions, and if you feel no emotion for a poem, neither will your singers or listeners. But not all poems you love will make good choral pieces. Difficult philosophical poems, for example, are not good candidates. Choosing poetry is highly subjective, but I'll venture a few observations, keeping in mind that we are looking for texts that invite musical translation. (It truly is translation; the poem is being transferred from one language to another. Good translators respect the idiomatic and structural differences between languages.)

1. I like direct, simple diction. Singing is an elemental experience. The word "stop" is much stronger, simpler, and more natural than its more learned synonyms, "hinder," "cease," "desist." The poetry of the King James Bible, with its short Anglo-Saxon words that we have spoken all our lives, is much more natural and satisfying to sing than are revised, accurate, scientific versions. I stay away from even great poems whose language is obscure for any reason. If you have trouble understanding a poem when reading it, think of how impossible it will become when submerged in choral counterpoint. Complex ideas severely limit musical development because they are already dense. (Complex and profound are not the same thing; a poem may be profound yet simple.)

2. Short poems give a composer the most latitude for musical metamorphosis. Look at the *Messiah*: Handel broke up the long text into very short segments. "And with His stripes we are healed" is a five-page piece built on just seven words. Randall Thompson's "Alleluia" is one word. But I see

composers today choosing page-long texts for three-minute choral pieces. Has a law been passed against repeating words? Or do these composers believe that if the text is printed in the program, the audience won't notice the absence of musical continuity? (Some opera composers nowadays make the same mistake in relying on super-titles to keep the audience interested. Titles are helpful for older operas in foreign languages—those operas had musical integrity to start with—but super-titles do not supply *musical* drama where there is none.)

3. The poetic quality—imagery—naturally attracts composers. This, however, is obvious; I don't think many composers are apt to choose poems that don't "sound" musical. There may be such a thing, however, as too much imagery. I have rejected poems that had so many references to sounds, instruments, and noises that I was afraid music would be redundant. This kind of text sorely tempts the composer just to chase the words around. While there are brilliant exceptions, these texts don't often appeal to me. The only poem of this kind I have ever set was suggested by the commissioning chorus: "Pied Beauty" by Gerard Manley Hopkins. I was against it, but careful study of the poem gradually engendered enthusiasm and stretched my horizon. I was well aware, however, that with such a text I would have to be particularly careful to provide a musical structure to support all the jingling and jangling, so the piece turned out pretty well. This piece is the finale of my cycle *The Children of David: Five Modern Psalms*. (I chose to use a recurring long line as a kind of ritornello, a scaffold on which to hang the bursts of color.)

4. Poetic diction is related to, but different from, imagery. It is definitive in the poem and should be honored in the

musical setting. Fine lyric poets are masters of poetic diction. What composer could resist the inherent music in "Let It Be Forgotten" by Sara Teasdale (1884–1933), which I used in the cycle *The Winds of May*:

> Let it be forgotten as a flower is forgotten,
> Forgotten as a fire that once was singing gold.
> Let it be forgotten for ever and ever.
> Time is a kind friend, he will make us old.
>
> If anyone asks, say it was forgotten,
> Long and long ago,
> As a flower, as a fire, as a hushed foot-fall
> In a long forgotten snow.

(Poem from *Flame and Shadow*, first published 1920 by Henry Holt Co. *The Winds of May* republished 2003 by G. Schirmer, Inc., New York)

Because of the poem's simplicity and repetitions, a composer can build polyphonic music upon it without threatening the listener's comprehension and without obscuring the quiet but heartbreaking emotion of the poem.

I learned a good lesson about poetic diction from my father. When I was considering "Pied Beauty," he pointed out how effectively Hopkins had alternated short, fast sounds with long, slow ones, particularly in the line "Whatever is fickle, freckled (who knows how?)." Most of the poem glories in the quick sounds of "dappled things," making the sudden long sounds all the more effective. The composer must be aware of this kind of music *within* a poem and make the most of it.

5. Musical structure. Here we return to what I believe is the crux of the matter. I said earlier that to write choral works

with musical integrity our first task is to understand the several kinds of structure in the poem we are going to set. Structure in poetry can include the pattern of lines, meter, rhythm, or stanzas (couplets, tercets, quatrains) or the larger fixed forms, such as the sonnet, ballad, limerick, sestina, etc. You will also find invented forms, variations of fixed forms, and free verse. We must recognize these forms when we set them, but our musical form will best be determined by another kind of structure—what I have called the psychological or dramatic structure of a poem. (Granted that simple repetitive stanzas may sometimes require music that sticks close to the poetic structure, this need not be a restriction; good composers can conjure countless variations out of simple ideas.) To find this dramatic structure, we need to analyze the poem, observing the location of climaxes, of repose, of suspense, tension, changes of mood, returns to previous allusions or moods (with or without the same words.)

As an example, look back at Teasdale's poem "Let It Be Forgotten." Study it as if you were going to set it for chorus. Take note of all the elements mentioned above and anything else that strikes you as a clue for your composition. After you have done this, go on to the following observations I am offering about the poem's possibilities for music.

The poem, it seems to me, is permeated with sadness, resignation, acceptance, and, above all, a sense of the passing of time: "forgotten," "forever and ever," "time . . . will make us old," "long and long ago," "long forgotten snow"—these are all of a piece. The first four words, "Let it be forgotten," form the motif of the poem. To an unusual degree, this motif suffuses the entire work and suggests the use of some *musical* motif—one with the potential for variation. I would also consider the use of one of the old modes to convey and heighten the sense of a bygone time. (I used Phrygian.)

The first three lines of the poem belong together; they are enlargements of the motif. Beginning with the second half of the first line, "as a flower is forgotten," this section seems to call for lyrical expression because of the alliteration, the flowing vowels, and particularly the phrase "singing gold." Modulation might direct the flowing movement toward a new musical goal. An imitative texture could be derived from the motif, giving the composer an opportunity for a gentle rise and fall in the vocal range and dynamics.

The fourth line, however, is very different in its diction. The flowing movement stops. Read it aloud and you will see that its sounds are longer. "Time is a kind friend, he will make us old." This does, indeed, require more time and demands a new musical treatment. It is a chance for variety, but you do not have to give up unity. You can change the texture but retain some important element of the first section—a rhythmic pattern, for instance—or continue the atmosphere of the old modality. This fourth line is also a summing-up of the first stanza; it suggests a full cadence—most definitely not a half cadence—but not in the home key. Is there anything remarkable about the first line of the second stanza, "If anyone asks"? This strikes me as the only time the author steps outside her omniscient point of view and becomes personal for a brief, but revealing moment. One voice part could sing this line alone. The final words of the line, "say it was forgotten," lead back to the motivic idea, but are not quite the same. This is a chance to return to the lyrical melody, perhaps with imitation, but varied. The elongation of the words "long and long ago," echoing the "ah" sound in "forgotten," is made to order for singers. It is also made to order for composers who are trying to unify their piece in the same way the poet has unified hers. It doesn't take a genius to see that these words can be set to the motif in long notes as counterpoint to the lyrical lines.

For the ending of the poem you have surely noticed that the poet brings back the flower and fire images, extending the "f" alliteration with "a hushed foot-fall." The last line of the poem, "In a long forgotten snow," returns to the key word of the motif, "forgotten." I have often said that Sara Teasdale must have loved music, because she made her poems so easy for composers to set. Here she has given us the opportunity for recapitulation of several melodic elements from the first stanza, as well as the golden chance to end our piece using the same motif with which it began.

Unfortunately, not many poems are so composer-friendly. And I hasten to add that my analysis is not the only one possible; every poem is open to different interpretations. I would guess, moreover, that most experienced composers make this kind of analysis intuitively. (Writing down these observations was harder than composing the music).

Whether the poem we choose is composer-friendly or not, the important thing is that we remain true to its psychological/dramatic form, rather than to its outer structure. No two sonnets share exactly the same dramatic structure any more than do two sonatas. By discovering the structure that lies *within* the poem, you will be well on your way to finding the right musical structure. Only when that becomes clear should the composer begin to write music. The music itself will alter, modify, and enrich your original concept, but rarely should you let it beguile you into giving up your concept entirely.

This seems like a good place to leave young composers—at work writing music with a good idea of the shape their work will take. They surely know, however, that their choral piece will not be judged by its *shape*, which will be as invisible to most listeners as is the steel infrastructure that holds up the concert hall. Nor will it be judged by its text. The piece will be judged by the beauty and the character and the originality of its melodies and harmonies and by the skill of the poem's translation to the choral medium. We wouldn't be composers if we did not happily accept that challenge. I hope that my suggestions may help my younger colleagues look at a poem as the framework for an imaginative musical form, not as a straitjacket. Choral composition should not be the musical equivalent of painting by numbers.

(Note: I later put words to the *Choral Suite* mentioned in the above article, being careful to retain the characteristic sounds of the original. But that's another story.)

D. Views from the Composer to the Conductor Pertaining to Score Study and Preparation

I work hard to write into the score all the information I can to bring about a performance as close to what was in my head as possible, but of course that is impossible. There are too many variables: size and reverberation time of the hall; quality of the singers and the accompanists; fallibility of my metronome or the way I felt the day I notated the tempo; the way the conductor feels the day of the performance (especially if I am the conductor). As most conductors know, this list could go on and on. Here's the bottom line: try it my way first; if that doesn't work, find a way that does. *Nota bene*: this does not include changing notes or making cuts.

E. The Relationship Between the Composer and the Commissioning Party

The following is a checklist I prepared for an ACDA panel.

Commissioning New Choral Music

Commissioning Agreement Checklist

1. **Identification of parties:** Is the contract between the composer and an organization, or between two individuals?
2. **Description of work:** Duration, number of parts, degree of difficulty, accompaniment, etc.
3. **Text:** Who chooses the text? Who is responsible for copyright clearance, if necessary, and for any fees involved in copyright permission? Usually copyright questions are the composer's responsibility.
4. **Premiere:** How long does the commissioning party have exclusive rights to performance? Usually this right is for the premiere only, but also sometimes for a stipulated amount of time after the premiere (to allow for tours, other performances, etc.). The composer should set a reasonable deadline for the premiere, so that if the commissioning party runs into difficulties, the work will not be tied up for years.
5. **Delivery date:** When is the score to be delivered? If instrumental parts are involved, when are they due?

6. **Payment:** Amount and method of payment. Usually the commissioning party pays half of the fee upon signing the agreement and the remainder upon delivery of score and/or parts.

7. **Extra costs**: The commissioning party usually pays for duplication of choral scores and the composer pays for furnishing instrumental parts as needed *if* the commission allows for this. The contract should state that the composer is to furnish good quality, legible score and parts. If professional copying or duplicating of score or parts is required, it should be decided in advance who will cover these fees. If the composer is expected to be present for rehearsals and/or the premiere, travel expenses should be figured into the contract.

8. **Ownership:** Commissioning a work does not imply ownership of it. The composer retains the rights of further performances, publication, etc. The composer also usually retains ownership of the original manuscript. The commissioning party is entitled to keep at least one copy of the score and sometimes a complete set of instrumental parts (which may not be loaned out) if this has been agreed upon. Use of these parts in the future with or without additional rental fees must be indicated in the agreement. (If the work is published, the publisher must be consulted about this.)

9. **Liability:** If the composer does not complete the commission, what is his or her liability to return the portion of the fee already received? If the commissioning party does not perform the work on time, or does not make payment when agreed, is interest to be paid to the composer?

10. **Recording:** The composer must approve the record label for a professional recording. A separate agreement (involving the

publisher in cases where the composer is under contract) must be made concerning mechanical rights. The commissioning party may ask for first refusal for commercial recording.

11. **Publishing and licensing:**

    a. If the composer is under contract to a publisher, the publisher may also have to be consulted concerning rental fees and other terms of the commissioning agreement (see numbers 8 and 10 above).

    b. If the work is accompanied by an orchestra that does not hold a valid ASCAP/BMI license, it must agree to secure an individual license for all performances of the commissioned work.

    c. The commissioning party should state in the agreement exactly how the commission credit line should appear in the published work.

12. **Legal details:**

    a. All rights not granted in the commission agreement are reserved for the composer.

    b. Amendments must be made in writing.

    c. A method of settling disputes should be written into the agreement.

(with thanks to Association of California Symphony Orchestras)

***

In actual practice, most commissioned choral pieces are usually agreed to more informally than this guide implies, but anyone contemplating commissioning a work (especially if it involves orchestra) should at least be aware of these potential problems. But the intangibles are just as important: knowing the musical style and skill of your composer and asking to see the text before he or she begins working on it.

This checklist does not mention a set fee because these vary greatly. When I was starting out I would write pieces for free. Later I had to make my living as a composer, and commissions were an important part of my income. If it is important to you that the piece you commission will be published by a major publisher, then you may have to pay an established composer's fee. Otherwise, why not encourage a young or lesser-known composer in the area? There are many excellent composers out there who are relatively unknown and would do their best to repay your confidence in them.

F. Views on the Teaching of Composition and How to Mentor the Young Composer

I have never taught composition and never will. While I have great admiration and respect for those who are able to teach composition without imposing their own taste and prejudices upon their students, I don't think I could do so. I have taught harmony, counterpoint, orchestration, and form and analysis; I believe that most students who want to study composition really need to master these skills first, and then they will be better equipped to develop their own musical ideas. I don't mean that students should not try to compose whenever they want to; one learns more by trying and failing than by waiting for some God- or teacher-given inspiration. However, I believe that all good composers are essentially self-taught.

A good composer needs two qualities that cannot be taught: creativity and an individual musical personality. At first, one learns by imitating the masters, but eventually every creative artist must develop his or her unique view of the world. "To thine own self be true."

Mentoring young composers is very different from teaching composition, of course, and as I remember my own longing for some experienced composer to give me guidance when I was young, I gladly advise young composers in whose work I see real talent. However, the best advice a budding choral composer will get will undoubtedly be from an experienced and sympathetic choral *conductor*. Better still is the advice Randall Thompson gave me: "Conduct your own works as often as possible." Nothing beats trying out your music on a real-life choir.

G. Individuals Who Were Especially Influential in My Development and Career

I have already mentioned the most important: my parents and Harold Schmidt, who was my choral mentor, boss, and lifelong friend. I was most fortunate to attend Stanford when the music department was young and small. The teachers were extraordinary. Most of my theory classes consisted of four students and were taught by Leonard Ratner, whose books on classic music have become classics themselves. He did not use textbooks in his classes; we studied only real music and learned about Bach Inventions by writing Bach Inventions, Mozart Sonatas by writing Mozart Sonatas, and so on right through music history. We had to get the styles right, and I later told Leonard that I could never have parodied so many styles in my comic opera *Tartuffe* without the training I received from him.

Sandor Salgo was a brilliant conductor, violinist, and violist; he was my first (and only) orchestration and orchestral conducting teacher. These classes were only one quarter long, but he put me on the right path, to become the best musician I could possibly be. Because of his advice I took up the viola and learned the C clefs by singing through the Paris Conservatory solfege books. Herbert Nanney, a fine organist, was my inspiring piano teacher at Stanford.

At Harvard I took composition classes from Walter Piston and Randall Thompson. Although there was little opportunity for private give and take, I learned a great deal from both of them and was encouraged to keep on composing. Later, I married Thompson's niece, Donata Coletti (her mother was the sister of Thompson's wife), and Randall Thompson remained an important and generous supporter of my music throughout the rest of his life.

I am, of course, indebted to an enormous number of choral conductors. Harold Schmidt gave the premieres of more of my pieces than anyone else. Among those who also believed in me from the beginning were Charles Hirt, Lloyd Pfautsch, Roger Wagner, Winifred Baker, Lynn Whitten, Bill Ballard, Royal Stanton, Bill Hall, Charlene Archibeque, and Richard Cox.

Besides this "old guard," there are happily so many other choral conductors with whom I have formed close musical and personal friendships that it is impossible to name them all. In the orchestral field I was indebted to Josef Krips, the legendary Viennese conductor, who took a personal interest in me and my music as conductor of the San Francisco Symphony and later in London, and to Corrick Brown, who I believe is the only conductor to have performed all of my orchestral works. There are many others—chamber musicians, pianists, singers, and opera directors—whose friendships go back half a century and more, without whom my life would have been infinitely less interesting personally and rewarding musically.

I mentioned my wife before, but here I want to give Doe her due. We met in a chorus; she is musical to the core. For fifty years

I have been able to count on her good taste, her honesty, and her love. She has been my indispensable partner.

H. Ten Works All Choral Conductors at All Levels Should Study

I don't like this kind of question. Composers and conductors are always being asked to name their favorite composer, favorite piece, favorite singer. The best answer is probably to say who we liked yesterday, because we have no idea who it will be tomorrow. Many pieces on this list are obvious choices for anyone in the choral field; I also listed some smaller works from different periods to balance the eighteenth- and nineteenth-century blockbusters.

1. Giovanni Pierluigi da Palestrina: "Super flumina Babylonis." This is one of my favorites from the "Golden Age" of choral music.
2. Giovanni Gabrieli: "In ecclesiis." All conductors need to know this exciting period of Venetian antiphonal music; this piece sounds almost modern.
3. Thomas Morley: *Madrigals a 4*, 1594. A wonderful collection from the Elizabethan period, but any of the works of Morley, John Wilbye, Thomas Weelkes, etc. will acquaint you with the delightful madrigals of the English Renaissance.
4. J. S. Bach: B Minor Mass. Any comment is superfluous.
5. George Frideric Handel: *Messiah*. A good example of the old saying, "A masterpiece is still a masterpiece even if a million people say it is." How could you *not* study *Messiah*? You might also spend some time with *Israel in Egypt, Saul, Judas Maccabaeus*, or the pieces that changed my life at

that first choral rehearsal I ever participated in, "Or Let
The Merry Bells Ring Round" and "These Delights If Thou
Canst Give" from *L'Allegro*.

6. W. A. Mozart: Requiem. Proof that even a supreme genius
can deepen his art by looking back to another era, the
Baroque in this case.

7. Johannes Brahms: *Ein Deutsches Requiem*. G. B. Shaw, a
music critic in his early days, was a perfect Wagnerite and
panned most everything by Brahms, including the
Requiem. Much later in life he saw the error of his ways
and asked, "How was I to know Brahms was a genius?"

8. Both Claude Debussy and Maurice Ravel wrote pieces
called *Trois Chansons*. Take your pick—both are delicious.

9. Zoltán Kodály: *Te Deum*. It owes something to Anton
Bruckner's great work on the same text but is a marvelous
introduction to early twentieth-century excitement within
the framework of classic structure.

10. William Walton: *Belshazzar's Feast*. Difficult but worth it.
In my humble opinion, Walton is the most underrated
composer of the twentieth-century.

I. The Future of Choral Music

In March 1973 the Choral Journal *published an article of mine that
dealt with the present and future state of choral music. The* Journal
*reprinted it twenty-five years later in the March 1998 issue, and it still
expresses my views on the subject. I leave it to the reader to decide
whether the twenty-first century finds choral music in a much different
position than it was thirty-three years ago when this article was written.*

Alienation and Entertainment

"On Alienation of Audiences" was the title of an article by Paul D. Hilbrich in the January [1973] issue of the *Choral Journal*. I read this excellent piece with great interest, but I have to admit that at the end I was still not sure whether Professor Hilbrich was for or against the alienation of audiences. While as a composer I can only applaud his plea for more and better contemporary music on choral programs, I must say, with all respect to the seriousness of his intentions and the skill of his argument, that I believe if his ideas are not qualified they could alienate everyone in sight—audiences, singers, and eventually composers.

Dr. Hilbrich's basic assumption is that there are two kinds of music: in his words, "learned music" and "entertainment." He sees the role of the choral conductor as a "leader in the musical community," a "taste-maker," one who should see that his or her programs "confront the unknown qualities of modern thought." In his view "it is up to us to present that challenge and to educate, or reeducate" in order to get music "back in the position where it influences contemporary tastes and values."

These are noble phrases, and no one could deny that there is a good deal of truth in all of them. But there is also a distorted emphasis here that has cowed conductors and listeners for so long that I hope you will permit me to speak briefly in defense of the conductors and composers who see themselves first as musicians, not sociologists—as artists, not priests.

It is no small thing to be a musician. One who brings beauty, delight, and understanding to his fellow men is fulfilling not a lower but a higher purpose than "representing twentieth-century values and aesthetics" (whatever those are). There is a limit to what even music can do. Let us simply write, teach, and perform the most honest, profound, beautiful, and, yes, entertaining music we can, both old and new, and twentieth-century values and aesthetics will take care of themselves.

What is "entertainment" anyway? Are Brahms's *Liebeslieder* entertainment, or are they "learned"? Beethoven's and Schiller's *Ode to Joy*? Shakespeare's comedies, Bergman's movies? How about madrigals of both the sixteenth and twentieth centuries? Entertainment is whatever "engages and pleasantly occupies our attention." Would we rather our music did *not* engage our listeners' attention or that it be unpleasant? The fact that we sometimes want more profound experiences should not lead us to turn our values upside down by assigning a negative value to a very positive quality.

But by "entertainment music" Dr. Hilbrich probably means show and pop tunes. It is a misleading term, however, for the sin of these tunes is not that they are entertaining but that they do *not* entertain anyone who has developed much musical sensitivity and sophistication. Music your twelve-year-old daughter or son finds new and exciting strikes you as clichéd and boring. But if you want to see instant alienation, try telling your child—or your chorus— that what they should like is "learned" music. They will get your message loud and clear: serious music is by definition not entertaining.

The real problem here is how to develop this musical sensitivity and sophistication so that your singers will be entertained more, not less. As their intelligence and sensibilities develop, they will be satisfied (entertained) only by more intelligent and sensitive music. I would not presume to try to tell you how this development can best be encouraged, but Dr. Hilbrich is certainly right in this respect: it is not by appealing to the lowest instincts, which are catered to incessantly by the commercial world. If given half a chance, most young people eventually come to realize that there is more to life than a loud beat.

Is it then a "challenge" they need? Yes and no, but there is a misconception here, I think. Overcoming a challenge is not in itself a worthwhile goal. It may be a satisfying by-product along the way to the real goal—bringing to life an absorbing piece of music that happens to be difficult. And it is the same with Dr. Hilbrich's "confronting the unknown qualities of modern thought"; a fine philosophical concept, perhaps, but it's no goal for a musician. We certainly all want to expand our understanding and experience by trying new works and techniques— and novelty in itself has positive value until the novelty wears off—but the "confrontation," as such, is only a means, not an end. Anyway, I suspect that modern man is hardly panting after more confrontation in his life—a little more clarity, compassion, and humor might be more welcome.

I suppose I should be more grateful to Dr. Hilbrich for warning conductors that they "carry a tremendous responsibility to ensure the survival of artistic creativity in the twentieth century." I do sincerely appreciate his concern, but I detect a lack of faith in the music itself. He seems to be trying to sell it on moral or sociological grounds and to make the conductor feel it is his *duty* to promote new music simply because it is new. But art, like love, cannot be a duty. It may be a hunger, a thirst, a need, a desire, even a passing fancy, but never a duty. And is it a compliment to our music to consider it so feeble, so helpless, so incapable of speaking for itself?

If we composers cannot compel and involve singers and audiences on our own merits both emotionally and intellectually, are we worth being put on welfare? When he quotes Milton

Babbitt's article "Who Cares If You Listen?" I wonder if Professor Hilbrich agrees with Babbitt's conclusion: "The composer would do himself a service by total, resolute, and voluntary withdrawal from this public world to one of private performance and electronic media, with its very real possibility of complete elimination of the public and social aspects of musical composition." Talk about alienation! Thank God choral music, by its very nature a communal activity, has so well resisted the elitist, antisocial tendencies expressed by Babbitt.

In fact, a case could easily be made that the choral scene is the healthiest part of the music world today. It is far from perfect, of course; elementary and secondary school training is often minimal or inferior; technique sometimes overshadows content; programs too often are planned to impress either colleagues or the youth cult. Paul Hilbrich is right to ask that we try more often to express what *we* feel—not what somebody felt three centuries ago. But it seems to me there is more active participation in choral music today than in any other musical field. More vital literature is being demanded and written, and there is more attention to repertoire of all periods.

We now have a great deal of good scholarship, and a healthy amount of experimentation exists side by side with new music of the more continually evolving styles. (Compare this with the typical orchestral repertoire: 99 percent old masters and early twentieth-century classics, an occasional avant-garde piece to keep up appearances, and nothing much in between.) I think it is a little unfair to single out choral music as a "smoke-screen . . . representing the creative activities of a past age." American choral conductors today are performing more serious new music than anyone and need not apologize for their "role in society."

And while touching upon Dr. Hilbrich's remarks concerning roles in our society, let me respectfully disagree with his statement that "we are an age without an art that expresses our own times." On the contrary, we are an age with few spiritual values, and we have a perfectly corresponding art. But art should be more than a mirror—that is a modern concept that smacks more of the historian than of the artist. It is a puny art that does not try to rise above its environment, try to inspire, console, and show the better way.

Lest anyone read me wrong, let me say finally that I am not disputing Dr. Hilbrich's warnings against mediocrity. I am not advocating frivolous programs, backward-looking techniques, or music that avoids the great human emotions and tragedies, both old and new. Let us think of ourselves not as "leaders," but as musicians who wish to perfect our art and to share it with others. Forget about molding public opinion and public taste—and let's get on with the very difficult and important job of developing our singers' innate respect and love for integrity and beauty. We need never appeal to their lowest appetites, but at the same time we must not teach them to despise joy, spontaneity, or simplicity—in short, the best things in life.

J. Comprehensive List of Works for Choir
Chorus and Orchestra:

SATB unless otherwise noted. Bold-faced song titles are available separately.

Seven Joys of Christmas: A Sequence of Carols (14:00, ECS) SSA or
    SATB, soprano solo, chamber orchestra (minimum of 13 players),
    1964, 1. This Is The Truth 2. Din Don, Merrily on High 3.
    Joseph Dearest 4. Patapan 5. New Year's Song 6. Fum, Fum, Fum
    7. God Bless the Master of This House (Quodlibet)

Singing Is So Good a Thing: An Elizabethan Recreation (25:00, CFP) 1970–71, solo tenor or soprano, chamber orchestra (minimum of 13 players), text: William Byrd, includes dances of the period, 1. Praeludium 2. Corranto 3. Canzonet 4. Gigg 5. Pastoral and Catch 6. Variations on a Popular Tune 7. Villanella and Ballet 8. Lament 9. Ayre (Pavane) 10. Dialogue (Galliard) 11. Verse Anthem (Ground) 12. Postludium

Songs of the Slave (34:00, GS) soli: bass-baritone, soprano, from the opera *John Brown*, large or reduced orchestration, 1993, revised 1996, **1. Blow Ye The Trumpet** 2. The Songs of The Slave **3. Dan-u-el** 4. Dear Husband 5. A Speech by Frederick Douglass 6. Declaration

Speech to a Crowd (15:00, Nat) baritone solo, large orchestra, 1974, text: Archibald MacLeish, reduction for two pianos (rental)

The King's Contest (26:00) *Dramatic Cantata* (GS) soli: soprano, tenor, baritone, bass, chamber ensemble (11 players) or large orchestra, may be staged as one-act opera, 1961–62, revised 1972

Mixed Chorus, Extended Works:

SATB unless otherwise noted. Bold-faced song titles are available separately.

American Madrigals (16:00, CF) flute, clarinet, bassoon, violin, viola, cello, contrabass; or piano, 1975, **1. Kind Miss 2. He's Gone Away 3. Kansas Boys 4. Adam's Bride 5. New York Girls**

American Trio (7:00, GS) *a cappella*, 2003, 1. Fire & Ice 2. Richard Cory 3. "Sweet Spring Is Your"

Birthdays: Round Numbers (10:00, GS) piano, 2004, 1. Bridget at Ten 2. Turning Twenty 3. Is Thirty Young? 4. Forty Notes for Forty Years 5. Fiftieth Birthday Card 6. Advice on Turning Sixty 7. Is Seventy Old?

Choral Variations on American Folk Songs (14:00, GS) piano, 1995, **1. Skip to My Lou 2. Let Us Break Bread Together 3. Love and Pizen**

Christmas Past and Christmas Present (7:00, GS) piano, 1987, 1. Christmas Past 2. Christmas Present

Earth My Song (18:00, GS) piano, 1996, 1. I Could Hear The Least Bird Sing 2. Isle of the Dead 3. Rebirth

Five Centuries of Spring (12:00, Pre) *a cappella*, 1964, **1. Spring** (Nash) **2. From You Have I Been Absent 3. Laughing Song 4. Loveliest of Trees 5. Spring** (Millay)

In the Land of Morgenstern (10:00, GS) piano, text: English and German, 1962–63, **1. The Questionnaire (*Die Behörde*) 2. The Odor Organ (*Die Geruchsorgel*) 3. The Lattice Fence (*Der Lattenzaun*)**

Missa Brevis, "Trinity" (9:00, GS) *a cappella*, 2000, 1. Kyrie/Sanctus 2. Hosanna/Benedictus 3. Agnus Dei

Peace Motets (10:00, GS) *a cappella*, 2002–05, **1. By The Rivers of Babylon 2. Agnus Dei (Dona Nobis Pacem)**

Seven Joys of Christmas: A Sequence of Carols (14:00, ECS) keyboard or solo harp or *a cappella* or chamber orchestra, 1964, 1. This Is the Truth 2. Din Don, Merrily on High 3. Joseph Dearest 4. Patapan 5. New Year's Song 6. Fum, Fum, Fum 7. God Bless the Master (Quodlibet)

Songs of Wisdom: Sacred Cantata (33:00, GS) *a cappella*, soli: soprano, alto, tenor, bass, five motets preceded by plainsong recitatives, 1958–59, **1. The Song of Moses 2. A Love Song 3. The Protest of Job 4. A Song of Comfort 5. A Song of Praise**

Suite for Chorus (15:00, GS) *a cappella*, 2004, **1. Kum Ba Ya** (Spiritual) **2. Too Young to Marry** (Folk-song madrigal) **3. They That Mourn** (Requiem) **4. Papageno and the Prince** (Fairytale)

The Children of David: Five Modern Psalms (28:00, B&H) organ or piano, mezzo-soprano solo, 1971, **1. Psalm 2. Joy 3. The Song of David 4. Man of My Own People 5. Pied Beauty**

The Shepherd and His Love (8:00, GS) SSATBB, piano, piccolo, viola, 1967

The Winds of May (10:00, GS) *a cappella*, 1950–60, 1. The Tune 2.
Let It Be Forgotten 3. Over the Roofs 4. I Shall Not Care
(SSAA) 5. Song (Love Me with Your Whole Heart)

Three Madrigals (9:00, GS) *a cappella*, 1953, **1. Impromptu 2. Deny It
as She Will 3. Moral Precept**

Three Motets (14:00, GS) *a cappella*, 1993–94, **1. Gloria 2. Alleluia,
Amen 3. Cantate Domino**

To Music (8:00, GS) organ (or piano), various texts, 1997

Tourist Time: Five Satirical Choruses (9:00, ECS) piano, 1957, 1.
Tourist Time 2. Boston 3. Cologne 4. Texas 5. Rome

Two Christmas Ballads (9:00, GS) piano or amplified guitar, 1969,
revised 2000, 1. Christmas Carol (Teasdale) 2. The Ballad of
Befana (McGinley)

Winging Wildly (17:00, GS) *a cappella*, 1996, 1. Birds at Dusk 2. The
Caged Bird 3. Everyone Sang

Mixed Chorus, Shorter Works:

*SATB unless otherwise noted. Works not published separately are listed
only under the titles of the sets to which they belong. See Mixed Chorus,
Extended Works.*

A Choral Tribute, "To All Choral Conductors" (7:00, GS) piano, 1983

A Love Song (4:00, GS) SSATBB *a cappella* (*Songs of Wisdom*)

A Song of Comfort (5:30, GS) *a cappella* (*Songs of Wisdom*)

A Song of Praise (7:00, GS) with SATB *soli, a cappella*
(*Songs of Wisdom*)

A Wedding Gift (3:00, GS) piano and violin (or flute), 1979

Adam's Bride (5:00, CF) instrumental ensemble or piano (*American
Madrigals*)

Agnus Dei (5:00, GS) *a cappella* (*Peace Motets*)

Alleluia, Amen (3:00+, GS) *a cappella* (*Three Motets*)

Blessed Are They (5:30, GS) organ or piano 1998

Blow Ye the Trumpet (5:30, GS) piano, organ, or orchestra
(*Songs of the Slave*)

By the Rivers of Babylon (5:00, GS) *a cappella* (*Peace Motets*)

Cantate Domino (4:00, GS) *a cappella* (*Three Motets*)

Christmas the Morn (5:00, GS) *a cappella*. 1996

Dan-u-el (5:00, GS) baritone solo, piano or orchestra
(*Songs of the Slave*)

Deny It as She Will (5:00, GS) *a cappella* (*Three Madrigals*)

Forsake Me Not, O Lord (8:00, ECS) *a cappella*, memorial motet, 1964

From You Have I Been Absent (3:30, Pre) *a cappella* (*Five Centuries of
Spring*)

Give Thanks Unto the Lord (4:00, CFP) *a cappella*, 1953, revised 1959

Gloria (3:00+, GS) *a cappella* (*Three Motets*)

He's Gone Away (3:00+, CF) instrumental ensemble or piano
(*American Madrigals*)

I Will Sing Alleluia (2:30+, GS) piano, flute, optional percussion, 1973

Impromptu (1:30+, GS) *a cappella* (*Three Madrigals*)

Island in Space (7:00+, GS) *a cappella*, text by astronaut and A.
MacLeish, 1989

Joy (4:00+, B&H) mezzo-soprano solo, organ or piano (*The Children
of David*)

Kansas Boys (3:00, CF) instrumental ensemble or piano (*American
Madrigals*)

Kind Miss (2:00+, CF) instrumental ensemble or piano (*American
Madrigals*)

Kum Ba Ya (2:00+, spiritual, GS) *a cappella* (*Suite for Chorus*)

Las Americas Unidas (6:00, GS) SATB and SA (children), soprano
solo, two trumpets, glockenspiel, organ, contra bass, text: English
and Spanish, 1986, alternate version: soprano solo, SATB, piano
(SA and glockenspiel optional)

Laudate: Memorial Motet (5:00, GS) *a cappella*, 1979

Laughing Song (2:00, Pre) *a cappella* (*Five Centuries of Spring*)

Let All Mortal Flesh Keep Silence: Choral Variations (4:00+, ECS)
a cappella, 1951

Let Us Break Bread Together (5:30, GS) piano (*Choral Variations on American Folk Songs*)

Love and Pizen (4:00, GS) piano (*Choral Variations on American Folk Songs*)

Loveliest of Trees (2:00, Pre) *a cappella* (*Five Centuries of Spring*)

Lydia's Romance (4:00, GS) piano (*The Newport Rivals*)

Make a Joyful Noise unto the Lord (3:00, ECS) *a cappella*, 1951

Man of My Own People (6:30, B&H) mezzo-soprano solo, organ or piano (*The Children of David*)

Moral Precept (2:00+, GS) *a cappella* (*Three Madrigals*)

New York Girls (2:00+, CF) instrumental ensemble or piano (*American Madrigals*)

Papageno and the Prince (4:00, fairytale, GS) *a cappella* (*Suite for Chorus*)

Pied Beauty (5:00, B&H) organ or piano (*The Children of David*)

Praise Him, Sun & Moon (4:00, Nat) SSATBB, *a cappella*, 1951, revised 1971

Professor Nontroppo's Music Dictionary (5:00, Pre) *a cappella*, 1973, optional piano accompaniment available separately, text: Italian music terms

Psalm (8:30, B&H) organ or piano (*The Children of David*)

Psalm 23 (4:00, GS) cello or other bass instrument, 1973

Questionnaire—Die Behörde (3:30, GS) piano (*In the Land of Morgenstern*)

Rejoice: An Easter Psalm (5:00, GS) *a cappella*, 1997

Rules for Behaviour, 1787 (4:00, GS) piano, 1954

Shadows of the Moon (6:00, CF) piano, 1976

Sing All Ye Joyful (4:30, GS) piano 1966, revised 1991

Sing unto the Lord a New Song (3:00, GS) double choir, ST/SAB, trumpet, 1964, revised 1998

Skip to My Lou (6:00, GS) piano (*Choral Variations on American Folk Songs*)

Spring—Millay (3:00, Pre) *a cappella* (*Five Centuries of Spring*)

Spring—Nash (2:00, Pre) *a cappella* (*Five Centuries of Spring*)

The Lattice Fence—Der Lattenzaun (3:00, GS) piano (*In the Land of Morgenstern*)

The Lighthearted Lovers (4:00, GS) piano (*Tartuffe*)

The Odor Organ (4:00, *Die Geruchsorgel*, GS) piano (*In the Land of Morgenstern*)

The Protest of Job (7:00, GS) *a cappella* (*Songs of Wisdom*)

The Song of David (5:00, B&H) organ or piano (*The Children of David*)

The Song of Moses (5:00, GS) *a cappella* (*Songs of Wisdom*)

They That Mourn—Requiem (6:00, GS) *a cappella* (*Suite for Chorus*)

Time: Lines Found on an Old Bell at Chester (5:30, GS) *a cappella*, baritone solo, 1996

Too Young to Marry (3:00, folksong madrigal, GS) *a cappella* (*Suite for Chorus*)

Why Art Thou Cast Down? (4:00, GS) SAB, piano or organ, 1973

Treble Chorus:

Bold-faced song titles are available separately.

Barter (8:00, GS) SA, piano four-hands, trumpet or oboe, 1994

Blow Ye the Trumpet (5:30, GS) SSAA, piano, organ, or orchestra (*Songs of the Slave*)

Christmas Past and Christmas Present (7:00, GS) SA, piano, 1987, 1. Christmas Past 2. Christmas Present

Christmas the Morn (5:00, GS) SSAA, *a cappella*, 1996

Lydia's Romance (4:00, GS) SA, piano (*Newport Rivals*), 1999

Seven Joys of Christmas: A Sequence of Carols (14:00) SSA (ECS) keyboard or solo harp or *a cappella* or chamber orchestra, 1964, 1. This Is the Truth 2. Din Don, Merrily on High 3. Joseph Dearest 4. Patapan 5. New Year's Song 6. Fum, Fum, Fum 7. God Bless the Master of This House (Quodlibet)

Sigh No More, Ladies (2:00, ECS) SSA, piano, 1957

Sing All Ye Joyful (4:30, GS) SSAA, piano, 1966, revised 1991

The Winged Joy: A Love Story by Women Poets (16:00, GS) piano,
1963–64, **1. Love Is a Terrible Thing (SSAA) 2. The Message**
(SSA and mezzo solo) **3. The Cynic (SA) 4. A Farewell**
(unison) **5. Love Came Back at Fall o'Dew (SA) 6. Red May**
(SSA and mezzo solo) **7. You Say There Is No Love (SSAA)**

Men's Chorus:

American Folk Songs for Men's Chorus (9:00, GS) TTBB, piano, 1954,
1. Aunt Rhody 2. The Wayfaring Stranger 3. The Blue-Tail
Fly: baritone solo
Blow Ye the Trumpet (5:30, GS) TTBB, piano, organ, or orchestra
(*Songs of the Slave*)
English Girls (8:00, B&H) TBB, piano, 1971, **1. Jenny Kissed Me 2.**
Julia's Voice 3. To Celia
Shadows of the Moon (6:00, CF) TBB, piano, 1976
The Spirit of '76 (3:00, GS) TBB, piccolo and parade drum optional,
1976

Unison Chorus:

A Farewell (3:00, GS, *The Winged Joy*) piano
It Is Good to Give Thanks (3:00, GS) piano, 1973

Rounds, Catches, and Canons:

Birthdays: Round Numbers (10:00, GS) piano, 2004, 1. Bridget at Ten
2. Turning Twenty 3. Is Thirty Young? 4. Forty Notes for Forty
Years 5. Fiftieth Birthday Card 6. Advice on Turning Sixty 7. Is
Seventy Old?
Canon Law for Newlyweds (9:00, ECS) *a cappella*, a Sequence of three-
to six-part rounds and canons from Proverbs, 1965, 1. Hear Ye,
Children 2. Whoso Findeth a Wife 3. A Merry Heart Doeth
Good 4. Who Can Find a Virtuous Woman? 5. Who Hath Woe?
6. Love Covereth All Sins
Catch 22 (*and 21 Other Catches and Canons*, 30:00+, GS) two to nine
parts, equal voices, optional piano, 1966–1983, 1. The Question
2. Birthday Card 3. Housewarming 4. Housecooling 5. Catch as

Cats Can 6. Blessed Be Thou 7. Hirtengesang 8. Old Age 9. Old Jokes 10. Two Friendship Canons 11. Music Is an Elegant Art 12. Good and Evil 13. Ode to a Choir Director 14. Humpty Dumpty 15. Lament (Little Willy) 16. Five Parts Wine 17. The Donkey 18. Goodbye, Dolly! 19. Handy Pandy 20. The Woodchuck 21. Forty Notes for Forty Years 22. Catch 22

Epigrams and Epitaphs (28:00+, ECS) two to eight parts, equal voices, *a cappella*, 1951–63, 1. The Fiddler's Wife 2. Why Not? 3. Hannah Bantry 4. Puddin' Tame 5. Advice to Young Ladies 6. Agnus Dei 7. Since It Is Raining 8. Benedictus 9. Epitaph 10. Always Be Sincere 11. Introduction to Vienna 12. Who Comes Here? 13. An Old Lady of Tring 14. Leg over Leg 15. Epitaph 16. How to Write a Catch 17. Says I to Myself 18. Deedle Deedle Dumpling 19. A Tutor Who Tooted a Flute 20. Kyrie 21. A Farmer Went Riding

Lament for a Choral Director (3:00, Nat) Double catch for three equal men's and three equal women's voices, trumpet, cello, and/or other instruments, 1951–63

Publishers:

Boosey & Hawkes (B&H)

Carl Fischer (CF)

C. F. Peters (CFP)

E. C. Schirmer, Boston (ECS)

G. Schirmer, New York (GS)

National Music Publishers (Nat)

Theodore Presser (Pre)

james
Mulholland

A. Biography

J ames Mulholland (b. March 7, 1935, in Laurel, Mississippi) is one of the most performed and published of American choral composers, as documented by the major publishing companies (European American, Warner Brothers, Alliance Music, National Music, and Colla Voce Music), as well as ASCAP. From 1992 through 2006 he has received and completed 124 commissions, and he has written more than 600 compositions over the course of his career. He accepts approximately twelve commissions per year, which he must coordinate with his schedule of appearances at clinics, workshops, and conventions and his primary duties as professor of music at Butler University.

Mulholland is frequently commissioned to compose pieces for state conventions and honor choirs, including numerous works for National and Regional Honor Choirs of the ACDA and MENC. In 1996 he received the prestigious Raymond Brock Memorial Commission from the ACDA. He was named Louisiana State University School of Music Alumnae of the Year in 1995. In 2004 the ACDA established a $5,000 yearly scholarship in his name for a doctoral student pursuing a career in choral music.

True to Mulholland's Irish heritage, his music is influenced by the English school of lyricism, which emphasizes the beauty of melody and text. Many of his text settings have become so familiar that the poems are instantly identifiable, much like the lyrics of a familiar hymn or folk song. Through music, he desires to share the beauty of the great poets and give them the recognition and appreciation they deserve.

Mulholland graduated from high school at fifteen. After one year at Mississippi Southern University, he began studies at Louisiana State University, earning a bachelor of music in voice and composition and a master of music in voice and choral conducting. He then attended Indiana University as a teaching fellow, where he completed all coursework for his DMA in performance and literature. Mulholland was director of choral activities at Southwest Missouri State University for one year before accepting a position at Butler University in 1964 as director of choral activities, where he teaches composition, choral arranging, and music history to this day.

***

I was an only child. My father was a philosopher/business-man, and my mother taught school before she married my dad. I believe their mutual admiration of the arts was what drew them together, and when I was born their love for literature and music was passed on to me. My mother arranged for my musical training to begin at a very young age. She sought out the best available teachers; by the time I entered high school I had five different private music instructors!

My mother sang all the time, when she was doing the laundry or cooking, when she was upset or happy; it was a part of her alter ego. Mostly she sang folk songs or hymns. I had many of the hymns memorized when I started Sunday School just from hearing her sing them. It made a wonderful impression on everyone at church because I not only knew the words, but I could sing them in tune. I loved the attention that I received from this activity.

When our family made the extended car ride into town, my mother would start to sing, and my father would add in some harmony. Sitting in the back seat, I would pretend to play the piano on the seat in front of me. We had a marvelous time.

Of all of the things I learned from my father, his use of quotes was the most influential. One of his favorite activities in the evening was to read to me. He would share poetry or excellent literature much before I could understand its meaning. His voice, with its eloquent Gaelic accent, affected me like a drone in a bagpipe band. I remember being mesmerized by the sound.

Growing up in Southern Mississippi, I came to realize that my father was quite a character; he owned a barbershop, a cafe, and a laundromat. After an early career in baseball and boxing he became an entrepreneur businessman and a respected civic leader. He had a savoir faire that opened doors to the local banks, which gave him a means to provide for his first family. (His first wife had died in childbirth just a short time after his oldest daughter died in a tragic accident at the age of twenty. He was a single parent of two children for ten years before he met my mother, and by the time I was born my half brother and sister had left the nest.)

I started tinkering around on the piano at a very young age. My mother played hymns very well by ear, and I would climb up on the bench beside her and pound away. When I started studying piano, I completely frustrated my teacher. She would assign me beginning lessons of single-line melodies that required certain fingerings. I wanted to make the music sound like what my mother was playing and often added in a left-hand note or an altered rhythm to make it more interesting. While I liked the result, the teacher was upset that I was not playing what was on the page and actually encouraged my parents to find me a composition teacher. In our small town, that wasn't an option, so instead my parents started me on instrumental lessons. I studied trumpet privately, as well as voice and organ. The organ lessons reinforced my idea that "bigger is better" and ended my single-line piano career. I found copies of music I liked and would study the pieces until I could play them. It wasn't until I started studying composition that I understood the importance of sight-reading from the piano.

When I began the first grade in school, I was amazed to realize that not every child had received the background in music and literature I had. Within the first week of school I was moved to the second grade, and before the end of my elementary education I skipped another grade.

Most of my singing as a child was in the church. I began singing solos in church when I was only eight years old, and the emotion of the moment reached both the congregation and me. By age ten, I was singing soprano with the adult choir and was hired by the local Presbyterian Church to sing in their choir. I was paid two dollars a week just to sing! I thought I had died and gone to heaven. When I was fifteen, the choir director at my church moved away, and I was hired to assist the interim director; I later took over the entire program. That church experience allowed me to write and arrange material that was immediately performed. The affirmation of my music by the church congregation was wonderful.

We went to hear concerts in New Orleans every month. The accolades that those artists received raised the bar for me and led to numerous childhood daydreams of walking out on stage; I yearned to have that ability. I would go home and practice three times as hard after hearing any artist perform and receive ovations from hundreds of adoring fans who were mesmerized by their artistry. Music has opened doors for me all of my life. New Orleans continues to be a dear place to me. After my graduation from Louisiana State University, I spent the next twenty-five New Year's Eves celebrating in New Orleans, and I still do when possible.

I was fortunate to grow up in Laurel, Mississippi, a small town that truly respected the arts and music in particular. Laurel has produced some great artists: operatic soprano Leontine Price, the author of *Tap Roots*, James Street, and a plethora of less renowned artists. The town's appreciation of the arts is one of a kind.

Of the one hundred students in my graduating class, almost thirty of them had a "senior recital" in music. My recital was in 1950, and I still remember every song on that program. As I came out on stage in my tuxedo I saw all of my buddies on the front row. I opened with G. F. Handel's "Where'er You Walk." I mispronounced the last word of the second line, "Trees where you sit." After my nervous slip of tongue, my friends started doing cartwheels on the front row! Aside from that embarrassing moment, the recital was most memorable. In addition to singing, I played one of my piano compositions and accompanied one of my friends as he played *Carnival of Venice* on the trumpet.

In my senior year, I was admitted to Louisiana State University on a full scholarship. However, my parents did not want me to go away to college at such a young age, and arranged for me to attend Mississippi Southern University for a year while commuting from home. I began my studies at LSU the following year.

My music caused me to stand out in school, and just like at church, I adored the attention. The more I practiced, the better I became. It's possible that I pursued music because of ego as well as the personal joy it brought me. I was a shy person, and when I realized I could let music speak for me, I could let the bee come to the honey. Music made me feel special in high school and acted as an equalizer because I was two years younger that most of my peers.

Now, music is my life, but so is teaching. As a teacher, I have the opportunity to expound on what I love. I can share music with others through my compositions but also through my commitment to teaching. I love to get in front of a captive audience of students, look into their eyes, share my passion, and become an artistic model for them.

B. The Creative Process

Although I have studied avant-garde music, minimalism, serial composition, etc., I felt like I had found my voice very early in my career; by the age of twenty-five, I had found my niche. I don't know of a single artist, singer, novelist, or composer who does not have a sense of personal style. You can read two paragraphs of Ernest Hemingway and recognize his prose or glance across a room and immediately recognize paintings by Claude Monet or Vincent van Gough. Most musicians can identify a work by Johannes Brahms or Frédéric Chopin, or J. S. Bach after hearing the first two measures. My music is no exception; you only need two measures of Mulholland to know he is the composer. You may not like it, but you will know it.

My inspiration comes from being at the piano. When I am at work, there are no outside influences at all. I don't have to be in a certain emotional state; music itself is my aspiration. Beautiful sounds that express the text are my muse. When I read a text over and over again I hear music in my head. I automatically want to capture that music and make the text "mine."

My creative process essentially comes from experimentation. For me, being at the piano and starting the process is nine-tenths of the battle. If I can then apply my training and talent with some quality control, the desire to make something more beautiful, different, or interesting will lead to an accepted result. When a chef is in the kitchen with the pots and pans and all of the ingredients and spices, all that is left to do is to put them together and start mixing. As an artist, I too test to taste and taste to test for the most satisfying result.

My inspiration as a composer is simple. Every day I wake up and realize my goal is to seek and to make beauty using my creativity, just as an artist tries to make a painting more expressive using colors and tools of his trade. The trial and error process, however, is necessary. I put things in and take things out of my compositions and decide which ideas work best. I love the process.

I probably could do more work away from the piano, but I am so keyboard oriented, I am more comfortable composing when sitting at the piano. Give me some manuscript paper, a text, and sit me at the piano, and I am ready to go. I may work on one measure for four hours, or I might put down an entire verse. I am in no hurry; my only criterion is that I have to love what I have written once it is completed. I want to be mesmerized by what I hear. I am an old-fashioned composer. I still use a number one pencil and paper. I feel more connected to the score that way because I can erase and add notes as I see fit. I have never used the computer; I have engravers who do that for me. I figure out the harmonic and rhythmic structure at the keyboard and then transcribe it for instruments or voices.

Once a composition is completely written, my talent again comes into play. I approach my work as a trained and knowledgeable musician, but there has to be something on the page before I can start revising it using tools of the trade. I envy my colleagues who can put their finished product on a page and be done with it. For me, that is just the beginning. That is when I start tasting or stand back from the easel and look objectively at my work. I have to be willing to admit when the depth perception is just not there. I ask myself if someone could practice this music for months and perform it twelve times without losing interest because I want people to be moved by my compositions.

I tend to write in short spurts. I am more or less a quarter horse; I cannot plow the field all day. I compose four hours every day; I tend to write for two hours, take a break, and work two more hours. To do your best work artistically, it helps to know your limitations. Sometimes I will accept a special commission and will have to burn the candle at both ends, but this is an exception to my rule.

I tend to write rather ambitious accompaniments. My piano parts are challenging and resemble romantic art song accompaniments, not oompah chords to keep the singers on pitch. I like for the piano accompaniment to be interesting, perhaps with its own leitmotif. I tend to think of orchestral timbres when I write; thus, my accompaniments are in several octaves.

I love to write for French horn and oboe because they blend so beautifully with choir without adding additional vibrato. Early in my career I wrote a few pieces with French horn that became best sellers in the choral world, which led to several new commissions for choir and horn. Rumors developed that I write for French horn because I play myself or that I write the part for my wife to play. Truthfully, I don't play that well and I don't have a wife, so let's put those rumors to rest.

Composing is a process of quality control; I probably throw out half of what I write. I can become a bit rhapsodic, practically moved to tears during the creative process, but the next day can play the same passage and almost throw up. Emotional moments, especially the highs, need to be scrutinized. The scrutiny comes from academic training. We must hone our skills to discern what is good and bad, what works and what doesn't work. The creative process comes from your heart and your soul. The resulting beauty, however, requires discipline, which comes from the mind.

A composer should be his own best critic. As a performer, I know there were times when I did not sing my best, and as a composer, I find creativity responds the same way. Some days I simply cannot seem to get going. When I put my stamp of approval on a piece, it has to be what I really want. If it is not, then I have to be willing to back the car up and take another road. I accept that some days when I am writing I am the pigeon and other days I am the statue!

The truth is that I love my music. I dote on in like a parent and it doesn't bother me to say this. When it complements a moving text, I get a tremendous emotional high. Like a child, it is a part of you; your creativity is beautiful, regardless of what other people think. The real joy of life comes from painting the picture, not seeing it hung on the wall. Creative joy for me comes from the creative process, not outside approval.

C. The Relationship Between Text and Music

I never feel compelled to write my own text because too many beautiful words have already been written in many wonderful ways. I am talented with music but not with putting words together. So I use poems from the many great minds who have expressed themselves better than I could ever dream.

I have a folder that contains a hundred or more poems I am considering for my next composition. I love to read poetry books and frequently turn down pages to mark a poem that catches my eye. If I really like a poem I put a slip of paper in the book, and when I know that I love it a copy goes into my "magic folder." Occasionally I will have trouble getting permission to use a text, so I try to use only poems that are in the public domain because it is a huge process to get permission from an author or to get a publisher to respond in a timely manner. It takes forever. Two months is the longest I will wait to get permission, because I don't want to waste time that could be spent on composing.

When a poem is first recited, you miss much of what the poet is trying to say. Only by reading it over and over again, stopping in certain places and emphasizing certain words do you begin to comprehend what is being said. I think the composer does this for the listener when setting a text to music. They repeat certain lines and emphasize key words and phrases with longer note values and the creative use of melodies, harmonies, and tempos. The music guides the proper interpretation of the text and provides the advantage of instant replay and slow motion to ensure the "understanding" is correct. The music should not distract from the poem but act as a musical thesaurus for appreciation and understanding.

I consider my music to be an extension of the text. When I sit down to write, I want the words and music to become one entity. Poets find beautiful ways to express thoughts with rhyme, adjectives, and verbs the way a composer uses melody, rhythm, and harmony. I try to write a piece that adds emphasis to the text; my music acts as a conduit between the poet and the audience. Heinrich Heine said, "When words can express no more, music begins." The poem already exists as a beautiful painting, and the composer tries to frame it with the perfect blend of notes to pick up all of the color and ambience already there. There are two ways of spreading light, with a candle and with a reflective mirror. When I can take a poem, especially one that is not well known, and "reflect" it and give it greater appreciation, it is one of my sincere joys. If art reflects life, then life reflects art.

After reading through a text several times, I automatically get an idea about whether the tempo is going to be upbeat or somber. A text on love or nature, for example, has a different feel than one that is humorous. The tempo helps ensure the words will be understood in the proper ambience. As I read the text, I look for a natural scansion to the line. Some will dictate triple or duple meter, but not all texts have that natural scansion, so I try to shift the barlines as needed to bring out the innate flow of the text. Certain words stand out to me and need to be favored in the compositional process with a higher pitch or longer note value. Before I think about melody and harmony, I think about meter and tempo. I try to get into the mind of the poet to see what they perceive as the meaning of their text, which leads me to dynamic shaping. I try to emphasize lines in a way that allow for musical development.

Most texts seem to suggest a voicing, but I frequently am asked to arrange a piece I have written for different types of ensembles. I find that this different perspective actually gives me more colors to use. For example, "Heart We Will Forget Him" was clearly written from a woman's perspective, but I was asked to revoice it for a large men's ensemble to perform on an AIDS awareness concert. Now some men's choirs are performing the piece from my revoicing and changing "him" to "her." I don't know if Emily Dickinson would approve, but it still conveys the emotion of loneliness and pain she intended.

The music is subservient to the text, as the text dictates both the form and the style of the piece. The great art song composers Franz Schubert, Johannes Brahms, Gerald Finzi, and Peter Warlock always found a way to use the text as the driving force in their music. I start my compositions by singing the text in a variety of ways and emphasizing the words I have identified as important to the listener. Melody grows out of the established rhythm, and I use trial and error to find a melody that rings true to the text. Once I have found that melody, I feel like I am truly into the ambience of the composition.

I love to watch painters paint. They don't dip their brush into one color and throw it on the canvas; they put a mix of two or three colors on the canvas and then step back to look at the result. They repeat the process until finally they find the vision of what they have imagined in their heads. This is the way that I compose; I cannot put just one color on the page and say immediately that it is truly what I wanted because I feel that method lacks imagination.

I have waited a lifetime to set some favorite poems of my father. When I find the perfect occasion to put these texts to music, I often feel totally inadequate for the task. I cannot write music for the same text twice. Once it is published, I don't get a second chance, which makes me very apprehensive to decide I am prepared to rise to the occasion.

D. Views from the Composer to the Conductor Pertaining to Score Study and Preparation

Music has to go from the pen to the podium. When it is from the pen, it is one thing, but when it is on the podium, it is something else. I remember one of my teachers playing recordings of the first movement of Beethoven's Fifth Symphony by two different conductors. Arturo Toscanini and Bruno Walter both presented wonderful performances, but the Toscanini performance was almost two minutes longer. I think Beethoven himself would have had a difficult time saying which one he preferred. The podium has to speak, because the performance suffers if the conductor does not have some freedom to interpret the music.

I am a romantic, and I create in a romantic idiom that is neither Baroque nor Classical. If three measures of my music have the exact same tempo, the conductor has not interpreted my music correctly. The tempo needs some give and take to emphasize the scansion of the words. A metronome should only give an indication of the tempo. Giacomo Puccini is another composer whose music requires nuance and tempo shifts to bring out the text. While I tend to put my music markings in Italian, I am not afraid to write English commands such as "no breath" or "move the tempo" or "bring out the alto line" to clarify what I want. While ritard works most of the time, I sometimes write in "subdivide" before the actual ritardando in the music.

I have heard my compositions performed many different ways. I have liked some performances more than others, but I approve of all of them. Some performances have made me wish I had written certain sections a little faster or slower, for instance, because the interpretation seems to work better than what I originally conceived. I want conductors to have the freedom to express themselves when performing my music. The conductor's

133

imagination and interpretation of what the composer is trying to accomplish is vital to the creative process. After all, that is the freedom the poet has allowed the composer.

Keep in mind that a conductor's interpretation may be limited by the ability of the choir. If the conductor has to break a phrase to meet the performance needs of the ensemble, the composer has to be willing to give them that right. If a smaller ensemble has to rush the tempo a little to reach the climax with enough breath, this is better than singing to the end of the phrase with a less controlled sound. I would rather have a less than artistic performance of my music than no performance at all. I do not mind a group that tries to overachieve with music that might be just a bit out of their scope. They may not make the ideal sound, but I love that they are reaching for their highest expectations. Conductors give composers a sincere compliment when they choose to perform their music. "'Tis better to have loved and lost than never to have loved at all." To paraphrase, it is better to have performed and not have achieved perfection than to have never performed at all.

E. The Relationship Between the Composer and the Commissioning Party

During the last twenty years, probably 80 percent of what I write is commissioned music. I average eight to twelve commissions per year, but I am totally myopic in my composition process and can only work on one piece at a time. I like to schedule a commission about a year in advance of the absolute final date they can accept the music.

When I receive a new commission, the first thing I do is ask for the parameters of the work. If it is for a high school choir, I let them know that while the piece is going to be theirs, I will try to write something other ensembles can sing with success. If the commissioning group has a particularly strong soprano section, or a weak tenor section, I can certainly work within those guidelines. What is more important is the size of the choir and the event surrounding the commission. The kind of text and instrumentation they want to use is vital to the beginning process. After all, the commission is to showcase their ensemble for that occasion.

I am willing to work with almost any text the commissioning group has in mind, but I always need to have the final choice. If they do not have a text in mind, I have hundreds of poems in my folder I cannot wait to set to music. If none of those is appropriate, then I go back to my literature sources and submit three or four texts I think would be fitting for their particular occasion. Agreeing on the final text is a process of trust on both sides. Occasionally I ask permission to use a second-choice text. I need that license of freedom because sometimes a selected text simply will not resonate with me when I sit down to compose.

Because I spend so much time working on each piece, I often get asked how I know when a piece is finished. When it is done, every single note is exactly as I want it. There is an instant intuition that when I play it the last time, I know it is complete.

Once a commission is sent, I am done with the process. I may rearrange voicing or rescore an accompaniment for various instrumentations if needed, but the music remains essentially the same. Once I have given birth to a new piece of music, so to speak, I don't go back and wish it were a boy instead of a girl or wish for dark hair instead of light. I fall in love with the music as I have set it to the poem, and this does not change.

Maybe I spend too much of my creative energy by accepting so many commissions, but I am flattered to be wanted. The fact that people want to perform what I love to compose harkens back to the attention-hungry little boy in the Laurel, Mississippi, church choir who couldn't say no.

F. Views on the Teaching of Composition and How to Mentor the Young Composer

Creativity seeks its own level. Perhaps talent is hereditary to some extent, but I think a great deal is instinctual. In our formative years, we lean toward certain attributes for either the joy they bring us or because of certain abilities we possess. When a student finds the creative outlet that makes them the happiest, they should be encouraged to focus their attention on and become more curious about that endeavor. Early training is so important, and parents and educators should support young musicians as much as they can.

The most important thing any young person who is interested in music can do is to study the piano. Every musician needs this ability, or they will be handicapped, whether in the studio, in score reading, or teaching. The keyboard is the mother of all musicians. For every hour that a young person sings, plays the trumpet, or practices conducting, he or she should spend an hour studying piano.

My greatest regret in my early studies is that I received only minimal instruction on string instruments. When I write for strings, I have to go to colleagues and ask, "How can I achieve this effect on the instrument?" Composers must be able to put their thoughts on paper, and to do that they need to know the parameters (strengths and limitations) of the chosen instrumentation.

Vocal composers need to realize that not everything can be written *a cappella*. To write accompaniments, they have to know the capabilities of each instrument and how they can be used to support the voice or add color to the music. Knowing how to use instruments to complement a choral work is a vital skill.

Also critical is understanding how to work with text. When I recite poems during my symposiums or clinics, I am surprised by how little is known about interpreting poetry. Choral composers study music all their lives but have only minimal instruction in poetry.

Young composers can gain a great deal by working in small groups to compare their work; learning how others deal with text is particularly helpful. As a teacher of composition, I have learned to work with each person's talent. I don't want to teach my students to sound like me. I want them to sound like the individuals they are.

If students must sit through four lectures before they are allowed to put down a note, they tend to emulate what was said. I want my students to compose outside the classroom and bring it back in to share. Composing, however, is a creative activity; my father used to say, "To be original, one does not have to say that which has never been said before. To be original, one only has to say that which is truly in their heart." Art has to come from the heart and the soul, but the mind must be used to accomplish what the heart and soul want to express. Imagination may be more important than an innate musical intelligence. Some modern art seems to bypass the heart and live only in the mind. To me, art that is mathematic and sterile is not art. Music can be amazing without bypassing beauty.

Some contemporary composers ask listeners to learn a new language to understand the piece, but if you don't learn the language, you cannot appreciate their music. To me, this is rather self-serving. They come up with a new language for expression, but it has no impact because it cannot be understood by the audience. If I have a young student who wants to explore the possibilities of electronic music or altered sounds, I usually refer them to a colleague with more expertise in that area. We all have our preferred means of expression; mine is acute romanticism, and I try to pass it on to everyone! I promote music that is profound, exciting, inspiring, and beautiful but uses a language that already exists. I support and applaud that which is new; you have to be willing to accept change because that which stays the same never improves. I like new music, but I prefer when it is added to something that already exists.

It helps to think like a vocalist when interpreting text. The understanding of vowels and vowel placement as well as the limitations of breath adds to the writing process. Certain vocal phrases can stretch the limitations of the voice, and composers must know to let the voice rest before setting up the next vocal line. You do not have to be a great singer, but the ensemble experience of realizing that the voice is married to the text, vowels, and consonants as well as the emotion of the poem, helps to interpret the music. When writing vocal music, singers seem to handle the emotion of text better than instrumentalists. My heroes, J. S. Bach, F. J. Haydn, Franz Schubert, W. A. Mozart, Johannes Brahms, Giacomo Puccini, Samuel Barber, and Roger Quilter, were all boy sopranos. They sang early in their musical lives. I believe singing in a vocal ensemble is an absolute must for choral composers.

G. Individuals Who Were Especially Influential in My Development and Career

I had the opportunity to study with a wonderful composition teacher when I was in high school. Samuel B. Wilson had published quite a few pieces but had a nervous breakdown while working on his doctorate at the University of Cincinnati and had to come home to Mississippi. Musically speaking, he was a godsend to me. I was simply amazed by his abilities and knowledge. I think I was also a blessing to him because I seemed to open his eyes and gave him the inspiration to teach. I came to him with passion and talent and he knew how to direct it.

Mr. Wilson taught me from a musical standpoint. Every interval or chord that he taught me was put into the context of a beautiful piece of music from the piano or vocal literature. The tritone wasn't academic, it was musical. His presentation of the twelve augmented chords in a row in Puccini's "Madame Butterfly" was a truly sensual experience for me as a young composer.

My theory teacher at LSU, Frank Crawford Page, was from England. He was an inspiration in the classroom, and he worshiped at the altar of music. Any time you walked by his studio, day or night, you could hear music—and he was playing it on the piano, not listening to it on a stereo. You would hear Ludwig van Beethoven one night and Sergei Rachmaninoff the next. He taught theory the same way Mr. Wilson taught composition— by using music and scores to make it real and not abstract. To appreciate the taste of vanilla, you have to taste it in a piece of pound cake. To appreciate a certain chord or interval, you have to hear how it has been used artistically. You cannot write a love letter until you know how to spell, but you need to hear how someone has used those twenty-six symbols in the love letter to create something of beauty.

Frank St. Leger, also from England, was my vocal literature coach at Indiana University. He seemed to know every art song ever composed. If I ever had a musical "father figure," it was St. Leger. He had a passion for music that reached me on a deeply personal level. Regardless of the occasion, he had something profound to say in a way that it had never been said before. I performed five of my vocal compositions on my doctoral recital at IU, and when I met up with Frank ten years later, he told me that he still remembered the second piece on that recital and proceeded to sit at the piano and play it from memory. It was so touching for me to be associated with him through my music.

H. Ten Works All Choral Conductors at All Levels Should Study

1. **B Minor Mass by J. S. Bach.** Bach is the guru of choral literature. This is the model for learning proper interpretation of chorales. Here is affirmation that there is a God!

2. *Messiah* **by G. F. Handel.** All choral musicians must have this work as a part of their repertoire to learn proper vocal technique in dealing with vocal fugues and melismatic passages. This is the bread and butter of the profession.

3. **Requiem by W. A. Mozart.** Observe the subtle intricacies and dramatic use of sudden dynamic changes.

4. *Schicksalslied* **and** *German Requiem (II Section)* **by Johannes Brahms.** These will develop baton technique in conducting complicated syncopated sections.

5. *Carmina Burana* **by Carl Orff.** Orff requires a careful balance between instrumental forces and voices as well as clear pronunciation and controlled tempos.

6. *Elijah* **by Felix Mendelssohn.** This choral work teaches operatic interpretation of music in relationship to text. Maintaining the flow of drama between soloist and chorus is essential.

7. *War Requiem* **by Benjamin Britten.** Conductors need discipline for understanding the form and shaping the choral dissonances.

8. **Symphony No. 2 (last movement) by Gustav Mahler.** This piece teaches technique of controlling *crescendos* and *decrescendos* to reach a desired climax without allowing a work to become out of control and is the chance to experience heaven on earth.

9. **"The Best of Rooms" and "Alleluia" by Randall Thompson.** Ideal for learning the proper use of vocal blend, resonance, and tone quality in *a cappella* singing without sacrificing the intonation.

10. For voice leading, any of the choruses from the **Bach Cantatas.**

I. The Future of Choral Music

I am more pleased with the choral scene today than I have been in a long time. When I was growing up, Fred Waring and Roger Wagner were models for the choral art. Even in the pop side of music, The Four Freshmen, the Hi-Los, and other groups were making a living with tight vocal harmonies. Every Monday night, I would get together with several of my friends and listen to three programs that aired on the radio: The Bands of America, the Voice of Firestone, and the Bell Telephone Hour, all of which were devoted to good music. Each show had its own orchestra. I first heard American artists Eleanor Steber,

Lawrence Tibbett, Leonard Warren, Rise Stevens, and Jan Pearce on these shows.

Presently, the growth of children's choirs is a promising development for the choral profession. These community choirs are at the forefront of commissioning ensembles and are singing music I never expected to hear from such young people; they are begging for more. Probably one-third of my commissions in the past twenty years have been for children's choirs. The "light" part of their program, what used to be pop music, now features multicultural music instead.

Conductors at conventions seem to want to perform more new music. That sometimes is a bad thing because I go to an ACDA convention and yearn to hear Bach, Mozart, or Brahms, but the new music is good because it keeps composers on the front burner. Conductors are no longer content to pull out a piece from their music archives that a former choir director put in the files thirty years ago. Conductors want their choirs to commission a composition, and when a new piece becomes popular, their conductor or organization is listed at the top of the page, and they gain recognition with every choir that performs their commission.

Most professional choral organizations are growing. We now have stars in choral music that are considered to be among the best in the world. I think this began with Robert Shaw. Choirs from all over the country are always surprising me with their excellence. I can remember going to conventions thirty years ago and picking out three outstanding choirs. Now I go to a convention and have difficulty picking three choirs that are not outstanding.

J. Comprehensive List of Works for Choir
Mixed Voices:

A Dawn Song from ICantori Series, SATB, *a cappella*, CV12-50865

A Lad and a Lass, SATB, CV10-96700

A Psalm of Life, SATB, CV10-96805

Agnus Dei from *Missa Romantica*, SATB, CV10-96425

All Hail the Power of Jesus' Name, SATB with optional brass parts, CV12-50830

America the Beautiful, SATB (small brass ensemble, full concert band, or orchestra score and parts), CV11-20108

Behold My Love from *More Burns Ballads*, SATB, CV10-96920

Believe Me, If All Those Endearing Young Charms, SATB, CV11-20119

Benedictus, Hosanna from *Missa Romantica*, SATB, CV10-96430

Bredon Hill from *A Shropshire Lad*, SATB, CV12-50850

Bright Is the Ring of Words, SATB, CV11-20118

Canticle of Psalms, SATB with optional brass ensemble, CV11-20109; brass ensemble score and parts, CV11-20109A

Carol to Beauty, SATB with optional brass quartet parts, treble, CV21-20900; score and brass parts, CV21-20108

Charm Me Asleep: To Music, SATB, CV10-96740

Come Let's Be Merry from *Three 17th Century English Lyrics*, SATB, CV15-96890

Come Thou Fount of Every Blessing SATB with optional brass parts, CV12-50810

Come Thou Long Expected Jesus, SATB, Tetra/Continuo TC-966

Down by the Salley Gardens from ICantori Series, SATB, *a cappella*, CV12-50870

Down by the Salley Gardens, SATB, Helicon Music Corporation EA00472

Everyone Sang, SATB, CV10-96580

Fair and True from *Three 17th Century English Lyrics*, SATB, CV15-96900

Four Stanzas on Love, SATB, CV11-20102

Fulfillment, SATB, CV10-96670

Giving, treble and SATB, CV20-96740

Gloria from *Missa Romantica*, SATB, CV10-96440

Gloria, SATB, *a cappella*, CV10-96600

Green Grow the Rashes O, SATB, Helicon Music Corporation
     EA00446

Had I the Heaven's Embroidered Cloths from ICantori Series, SATB,
     a cappella, CV12-50860

Hail to Thee, Blythe Spirit, SATB, CV40-96790

Heart We Will Forget Him! SATB with French horn, CV12-50900

Highland Mary, SATB, Helicon Music Corporation EA00448

House o Life, SATB, CV10-96720

How Can I Keep from Singing, SATB, CV10-96685

How Can I Keep From Singing, treble and SATB, CV10-96680

How Do I Love Thee, SATB, Alliance Music Publications AMP0279

I Am Bound for the Promised Land, SATB, Tetra/Continuo

I Lived with Love, SATB, CV10-96320

I Remember, I Remember, SATB, CV11-20106

I Wish I Had a Shepherd's Lamb, SATB, Helicon Music Corporation
     EA00474

If Love Is What the Rose Is, SATB, CV10-96710

If Love Should Count You Worthy, SATB, CV11-20105

If Thou Must Love Me, SATB, CV10-96900

Keramos, SATB, CV10-96820

Kyrie eleison from *Missa Romantica*, SATB, CV10-96445

Kyrie eleison, SATB, *a cappella*, CV10-96510

Laugh and Be Merry, treble and SATB, CV10-96480

Let My Voice Ring Out, SATB, CV10-96590

Life Has Loveliness to Sell, SATB, CV11-20101

Lord, Thou Hast Been Our Dwelling Place, SATB, CV10-96690

Loveliest of Trees, SATB, CV11-20107

Measure Me, Sky, SATB with optional orchestra score and parts, CV21-20101

Mementos of Millay, SATB, CV10-96400

Missa Romantica, SATB with optional orchestra or chamber ensemble, CV10-96450

Music, SATB, CV10-96850

Music, When Soft Voices Die, SATB, CV10-96410

My Jesus, I Love Thee, SATB with optional brass parts, CV12-50820

My Old Kentucky Home, SATB, CV10-96910

No Other Gifts, SAB, CV21-20401

O Whistle and I'll Come from *More Burns Ballads*, SATB, CV10-96930

O Wondrous Type, O Vision Fair, treble and SATB, CV40-96740

Ode to Music, SATB, with optional brass and percussion ensemble score/parts, CV10-96950

Oh See How Thick the Goldcup Flowers (from *A Shropshire Lad*), SATB, CV12-50840

On Our Journey to the Kingdom, SATB with optional brass parts, CV12-50800

Our Love Is a Song, SATB, with tenor solo and optional brass quartet, CV10-96540

Psalm 23 (from *Canticle of Psalms*), SATB, CV11-20110

Psalm 27 (from *Canticle of Psalms*), SATB, CV11-20113

Psalm 84 (from *Canticle of Psalms*), SATB, CV11-20112

Psalm 98 (*O Sing unto the Lord*) SATB with optional horn, CV10-96330

Psalm 103 (from *Canticle of Psalms*), SATB, CV11-20111

Red, Red Rose, SATB, Helicon Music Corporation EA00445

Sanctus from *Missa Romantica*, SATB, CV10-96435

Schule Aroon (*Come O Love*), SATB, Helicon Music Corporation EA00473

Shall I Compare Thee to a Summer's Day, SATB, Alliance Music Publications AMP0142

Songs of America, SATB, Hope Publishing/Somerset Press SP 418

Take up the Song (from *Mementos of Millay*), SATB, CV10-96395

That I Shall Never Look upon Thee Moré, SATB, Alliance Music
   Publications AMP0147

The Banks o' Doon, SATB, Helicon Music Corporation EA00447

The Breath of God, treble and SATB, CV10-96500

The Carols of Christmas, SATB, Neil A. Kjos Music Company GE48

The Darkling Thrush, SATB, CV13-96900

The Greatest of These Is Love, SATB, 1CV0-96520

The Wild Honeysuckle, SATB, CV10-96800

The Winter Is Past from *More Burns Ballads*, SATB, 10-96940

There Is a Vale Which None Hath Seen, SATB, CV10-96630

There Is God, SATB, CV10-96360

Think on Me, SATB, CV20-96895

This Is My Letter to the World, SATB, CV11-20100

Thou Art My Life, My Love, My Heart, SATB, CV10-96660

Three American Folk Hymns (not yet available), SATB, brass ensemble, CV10-96860

Timeless, SATB, CV10-96460

Tis a Little Journey, SAB, CV10-96610

Today, SATB with optional orchestra score/parts, CV10-96560

Two Irish Aires, SATB with tenor solo CV10-96695

We Are the Music Makers, SATB, wind ensemble score/parts,
   CV10-96352

We'll Go No More A-Roving, SATB, CV11-20115

What Lips My Lips Have Kissed from *Mementos of Millay*, SATB,
   CV10-96370

When I Lay Me Down to Sleep from *Three 17th Century English Lyrics*,
   SATB, CV15-96880

When We Two Parted, SATB, CV11-20114

White in the Moon (from *A Shropshire Lad*), SATB, CV12-50835

Will You Teach Your Children What We Have Taught Our Children,
   SATB, CV20-96625

With Rue My Heart Is Laden from *A Shropshire Lad*, SATB, CV12-50845

You, Rose of My Heart, SATB, CV11-20104

Women's Choir:

A Psalm of Life, SSA, CV10-96810

At the Heart of Music, SSA, CV10-96570

Caledonian's Air, SSA, CV21-20220

Carol to Beauty, SSAA, optional score and brass parts, CV21-20232

Children, SA, CV18-96900

Come Let's Be Merry (from *Three 17th Century English Lyrics*), SSA, CV20-96840

Come My Little Children, SSA, CV10-96530

Diary of Dickinson, SA, CV10-96840

Each and All, SSA, Alliance Music Publications AMP0216

Fair and True (from *Three 17th Century English Lyrics*), SSA, CV20-96850

Footprints on the Sands of Time, SA, CV10-96770

For a Child, SSA, CV10-96650

Give Us Love, Give Us Peace, SSA, CV10-96470

God Bless You (from *Three Anonymous Blessings*), SA, CV20-96710

Green Grows the Laurel from *Three Anonymous Irish Love Songs*, SSAA, CV10-96870

Heart We Will Forget Him! from *Three Love Songs*, SSA with French horn, CV12-50890

Hey Ho, the Morning Dew from *Three Anonymous Irish Love Songs*, SSAA, CV10-96880

How Can I Keep From Singing, SSA, CV10-96675

Hungering Hearts, SSAA, CV10-96790

Hymn of Life and Love, SSA, CV18-96820

I Could Not Let You Go from *Mementos of Millay*, SSAA, CV10-96390

I Will Walk with My Love from *Three Anonymous Irish Love Songs*, SSAA, CV10-96890

Joy, SSA, CV21-20237

Life Has Loveliness to Sell, SSA, CV11-20200

Life Owes Me Nothing, SA, CV10-96730

Loch Lomond, SSA, CV21-20223

Love Alters Not, Sonnet 116, SSA, CV10-96420

Love Will Find Out the Way, SSA, CV11-20201

Love's a Lovely Lad, SSA, CV11-20201

Measure Me, Sky, SSA, CV21-20202

Moments of Being, SSA with optional brass quintet score/parts, CV10-96340

Nobody Knows This Little Rose from *Three Love Songs*, SSA, CV12-50880

Portraits by a Neighbor from *Mementos of Millay*, SSAA, CV10-96380

Reeds of Innocence, SSA, CV21-20201

Seasons of Life, SA, CV20-96760

Shall I Compare Thee to a Summer's Day, SSAA, Alliance Music Publications AMP0143

So I Let Him Lead Me Home (from *Three Love Songs*), SSA, CV12-50885

Spirit of Delight, SSA, CV10-96640

Sunshine and Music from *Three Anonymous Blessings*, SA, CV20-96730

Thanks Be to Thee, SA, CV10-96830

The Fairest Day, SA, CV10-96750

The Needs of the World from *Three Anonymous Blessings*, SA, CV20-96720

There Was an Old Farmer, SSA, CV21-20203

Think on Me, SA, CV20-96900

Thoughts on Music, SSA, CV10-96490

When I Lay Me Down to Sleep from *Three 17th Century English Lyrics*, SA, CV20-96830

Where Dwells the Soul of My Love, SSA, CV11-20203

Wi' a Hundred Pipers, SA with optional score/brass quintet parts, CV21-20224

Widmung, SA, CV20-96880

Will You Teach Me, SA, CV10-96550

Will You Teach Your Children What We Have Taught Our Children, SA, CV20-96630

Men's Choir:

Green Grow the Rashes O, TTBB, Helicon Music Corporation EA00815

Heart We Will Forget Him! TTBB with French horn, CV12-50895

Highland Mary, TTBB, Helicon Music Corporation EA00817

How Do I Love Thee, TTBB, Alliance Music Publications AMP0149

If Still Your Orchards Bear from *Mementos of Millay*, TTBB, CV10-96385

Passing By, TTBB, *a cappella*, CV10-96780

Psalm 103 (from *Canticle of Psalms*), TTBB, CV11-20301

Red, Red Rose, TTBB, Helicon Music Corporation EA00814

That I Shall Never Look Upon Thee More, TTBB, Alliance Music Publications AMP0148

The Banks o' Doon, TTBB, Helicon Music Corporation EA00816

Think on Me, TTBB, CV20-96905

When I Fall in Love, TTBB, CV11-20300

Winter Night from *Mementos of Millay*, TTBB, CV10-96375

john
Rutter

A. Biography

John Rutter was born in London in 1945 and received his first musical education as a chorister at Highgate School. He went on to study music at Clare College, Cambridge, where he wrote his first published compositions and conducted his first recording.

Rutter's composition career has produced both large- and small-scale choral works, orchestral and instrumental pieces, a piano concerto, two children's operas, music for television, and specialist writing for such groups as the Philip Jones Brass Ensemble and the King's Singers. His most recent large choral works—*Requiem* (1985), *Magnificat* (1990), *Psalmfest* (1993), and *Mass of the Children* (2003)—have been performed many times in Britain, North America, and a growing number of other countries. He coedited four volumes in the *Carols for Choirs* series with Sir David Willcocks and, more recently, has edited the first two volumes in the Oxford Choral Classics series, *Opera Choruses* (1995) and *European Sacred Music* (1996).

From 1975 to 1979 Rutter was director of music at Clare College, whose choir he directed in a number of broadcasts and recordings. After giving up the Clare post to allow more time for composition, he formed the Cambridge Singers as a professional chamber choir dedicated primarily to recording. He now divides his time between composing and conducting. Rutter has guest conducted or lectured at many concert halls, universities, churches, music festivals, and conferences in Europe, Scandinavia, North America, and Australasia. In 1980 he was made an honorary Fellow of Westminster Choir College, Princeton, and in 1988 he was named a Fellow of the Guild of Church Musicians. In 1996 the Archbishop of Canterbury conferred a Lambeth Doctorate of Music upon him in recognition of his contribution to church music, and in 2007 he was honored with a CBE for his services to music.

In 1984 Rutter formed his own record label, Collegium, with the aim of bringing choral music to a wider audience through performances of the highest possible quality. Collegium has garnered great success and wide acclaim over the years. Rutter commented, "There was a much larger audience worldwide for the sort of music we were recording than we had ever known. It's really, really heartening, because it shows that choral music is much closer to the center of people's affections than is often suspected." In addition to showcasing Rutter's own work, including his beautiful *Requiem* (1998), Collegium CDs feature a wealth of traditional and sacred music.

John Rutter's music is published by Oxford University Press and by Hinshaw Music, Inc.

***

I began singing and playing piano before I knew how to read music and before I ever took part in any group musical activity. When I was four or five years old, I climbed up to the piano that stood in my parents' apartment. They never used it because neither of them were musicians. The piano was only there because the previous occupants had left it behind—they probably could not get it back down the stairs. I used to play and improvise on that piano for hours on end, singing in my little treble voice.

When I was about seven years old, a family friend heard me sing and asked my parents if they had considered having me audition for one of the cathedral choirs; she suggested St. Paul's Cathedral in London. That certainly would have set me on an interesting path had my parents pursued it, but I really did not want to take the audition and my parents did not push me. Students in a cathedral choir school have to board on the premises and cannot come home every day. I did not want to live away from home and my parents, perhaps wisely, agreed.

Instead they sent me to Highgate School in North London, a boys' school that I could attend while living at home. It had an excellent chapel choir and high levels of musical activity. My main musical experiences came from that school and from a local church choir I joined in my teens.

The Highgate Choir not only sang every day in the school chapel but was also called on to sing in London performances of several of the symphonic works that have parts for boys' choir. We sang in Carl Orff's *Carmina Burana* and the Mahler Third and Eighth Symphonies, which gave me my first taste of making music at a professional level. As children, we were making music at a very high level alongside adults in both the orchestra and the choir. I was thrilled by these experiences. Taking part in such high-caliber music at a young age gave me a taste for performance that I have retained ever since.

Composition was encouraged at Highgate, which was not a common practice in all of the schools at that time. A number of us were scribbling down our first efforts on paper and giving little performances at school. I was one of a number of composers in that group, which included John Tavener (now Sir John Tavener). We grew up together and had our lessons with the same inspirational teacher, Edward Chapman, which proved to be quite a formative experience. So, in a way, music chose me; I didn't choose it.

Perhaps the high point of those formative years was taking part in the Benjamin Britten *War Requiem*, which was recorded under the baton of the composer in 1963. Both John Tavener and I sang in the boys' choir. Although our voices had changed by then, we managed to fake enough of a falsetto voice to stay in the choir and have this remarkable opportunity to sing in what has become a historic recording. It was a thrill for us both. I think Chapman allowed us to do it because he knew we would learn from the experience and because he needed some good sight-readers in the alto section.

Much of my composing and conducting activity has been in the choral area, which happened by accident. I think I would have been happy as an orchestral composer or opera conductor, but my foundation in choral music has caused about 80 percent of my compositional output—and my conducting—to be choral as well. That was never the plan, but when I write for or direct a choir, I feel that I am returning to my earliest musical roots.

Composing for me is a compulsion. There is no real rhyme or reason for what calls me to put my ideas on paper. It has always seemed a natural thing to do, and perhaps the most crucial thing is that nobody has ever stopped me. My parents had confidence in me and trusted my instincts, and only as an adult do I realize what a remarkable thing that was. The thing that parents of people who want to go into the arts so often say is, "Oh dear, it would be much better for you to be a doctor or lawyer. You don't want to be a starving musician."

No one ever told me what a difficult and precarious career composing can be economically and professionally or ever said, "Don't do it," which is why I suppose I am still at it. I can't claim that I have had a hard life and early struggles. In terms of my place in the world, I was fortunate to get my pieces into print at an early age, which was quite helpful.

When I left high school to study music at Cambridge, I encountered many fine musicians, and no negative peer pressure. While I was a student, Sir David Willcocks, who was then the director of King's College Choir, heard about and asked to see some of my work. He then brokered a deal with Oxford University Press for my first bundle of compositions, which included the *Shepherd's Pipe Carol*. I was twenty-one years old at the time, and Oxford University Press has been my primary publisher ever since.

My composition teacher at Cambridge was a gifted young composer, who was maybe only six or seven years older than I was, named Patrick Gowers. His career has focused on writing movie and television music. Thanks to his example, I grasped the essentials of writing for TV, so I was fairly well equipped when the opportunity came along. Everything in those settings is done with a "click track," and the music is laid down to enhance the drama and the atmosphere in the pictures. I found that type of writing very stimulating and would have liked to do more of it, but I chose to walk away from my television work in the mid 1970s because I accepted the position of director of music at Clare College. Writing for television proved to be one thing too many.

People who specialize in film and TV music often make that their life's work—although it was not always the case. If you think back to the days of the Hollywood greats, composers such as Erich Korngold composed music in many styles, including quite a bit of concert music. I found that I gravitated toward my everyday activities, namely directing the choir at Clare College and accepting an increasing number of commissions for choral compositions. It was an exciting time in my life, but in the end the road of television and film composition was one I simply could not take.

The other road I never followed was musical theater. I adore the stage and would love to have been involved in writing operas or musicals, but neither of these has happened. Maybe it isn't too late to begin! In both cases, though, my love of the voice would have directed me to what I might have written. But the thing about musical theater, if not opera, is that it does not stand or fall on its music but rather on its dramatic idea. With musicals, the book definitely comes first. A number of shows with fine music have never achieved popular acclaim because the book was wrong. If I had found the Oscar Hammerstein of my dreams to collaborate with, then I might have followed the path of musical theater. That genre requires a huge investment of time and effort, and I could not start writing for it without the right idea. While I regret that I have not explored that medium more, I am grateful for all the opportunities that have come my way in choral music.

B. The Creative Process

The text is the starting point in choral music. For me, finding the right text takes me halfway to completing a composition. If the words are wrong, then it is an uphill battle all of the way. I think that most other choral composers would say the same thing.

The exception is when I write my own text. I perhaps start with a fragment of phrase and a piece of the text and build it up, brick by brick, sort of like a mosaic. . . . When I add a music tile, more word tiles will come. For me, the music and text tend to grow together when I write my own lyrics.

The first thing I do when I set a preexisting poem or text to music is to write it out by hand because it helps me get inside the text and make it my own. I develop a better understanding of the structure and its key points. The structure of the musical composition is often inspired by the structure of the words. A good case in point is my *Gloria*. This three-movement composition corresponds word for word with the three-part text structure. The first movement is declamatory and joyful, the second movement is a prayer, and the third movement is again joyful and closes with an extended "amen."

When searching for ideas, I sometimes sit and jot down melodic fragments and shapes and manipulate them in all kinds of ways, like inverting the intervals or turning them backwards or expanding them and playing with rhythmic structures to see where they might lead me. The art of composition is to stretch these little bits of raw material out to fill a time scale. Visual artists like sculptors and painters don't have to deal with time; this problem exists solely in music.

While music exists in time, inspiration is usually just a lightning flash, and a flash of lightning does not a concert make. Music has to occupy the time slot needed to express the idea. In a way, a composer is stretching out a ball of chewing gum into a long string of gum. It is a technical and, in the literal sense, an artificial process because the composer must use both artifice and skill. That "stretching" is the real hard slog of my composing. As for getting the idea in the first place—well, nobody really knows where ideas come from. I can have bad days when nothing usable comes and good days when quite a bit of material may come my way. After that brief inspiration, the rest is all manipulation and technique. However, during the process of manipulating musical ideas, new ideas do seem to come along. Stravinsky may have put it best; when asked, "When do your ideas come to you?" he replied, "When I am working." I think that sums it up.

Consider the novelist who writes 1,000 words per day because that is what the work requires and who won't cover up the typewriter until that quota is complete. I don't have a set number of measures that I write every day, but I do try to keep fixed hours. If I waited until I felt like writing, I might wait forever. Professional composers must have a routine. In my case, bottom hits seat at about 9:30 in the morning and, with meal breaks, I generally work until midnight before I call it a day. Most of the first couple of hours is spent cranking up the motors. I can't nibble and peck at a composition in just a couple hours a day—that stretches the process out too long. I find I waste time if I try to write a composition in short bursts. For me, it is better to sit down and stick with it.

Because I have numerous other responsibilities as a conductor and with my record company, I try to alternate between one activity and the next. Conducting dates tend to happen when they happen and I cannot always schedule set periods of composing time in between. I do try to space out my conducting and my recording activities, but the reality is that composition tends to get squeezed into the cracks of my schedule because conducting and running the record label tend to stake the first claim on my time. I have to make a concerted effort to leave at least one month a year free to devote to nothing but writing. I regret that I don't spend more weeks in the year composing; I probably only spend a total of two or three months of the year actively writing. Back in the 1980s it seemed like I was always on a plane headed from one place to the next, but I am trying now to travel less and devote more time to my compositions.

I am fascinated with performing and recording music, and that feeds into my compositions. I think I would have been happy in the eighteenth century with a job like Haydn's. His job at Eszterháza involved conducting and directing a performance one moment, sitting down to supper with his colleagues in the orchestra the next moment, then taking off to write next week's symphony. For me, composition and performance go hand in hand. I couldn't live a life in which I didn't perform, it is that important to me.

Composition is a solitary activity that cannot be done when other people are around. I seclude myself when I am writing because I need the peace and quiet. But because I am quite a sociable fellow, I also enjoy making music when I get together with other people because I thrive off their insights and energy, and the good things that flow from being with other musicians and making music. Both are important to me.

As I look at the full score of a finished piece, I hear a perfect tape of the piece playing in my head. The composer has to be able to do that; what is on the page is just a graph of the sounds in the composer's head. Most composers go to great efforts to put down as accurately as possible on paper what they want to hear. It will never be perfect because translating sound into little blobs on a page is an approximation at best. No matter how exact you try to be, the space "between the notes," which cannot be notated, will always remain. This is the imponderable element, the magic, the atmosphere, the mood that can only be captured by performing the music.

C. The Relationship Between Text and Music

The hardest thing I do as a composer is to find the text and identify its ideal musical structure. I have found over the years that the correct sound medium tends to present itself if I am patient enough and, almost always, my first thoughts are the best thoughts. When I have been asked to adapt pieces, such as a mixed choir piece for treble voices, it may work alright, but generally it is not as good as the original. Compositional ideas usually find their correct sound medium one way or another. It is a mysterious but instinctive process, and I have found that I have to trust it when it happens.

I tend to use my own lyrics only if I cannot find anything else that works. I would much rather set a classic or preexisting text. Sometimes, for example in the case of *Look at the World*, I get invited to write a piece for a particular occasion. In this instance, it was for the fiftieth anniversary of an ecological organization in England that works to preserve the countryside and the rural habitat. I couldn't find a suitable text in the Bible (or anywhere!) on the theme of mankind's obligation to the environment or to protecting our planet, so I was obliged to write my own text.

My home is only fifteen minutes away from the Cambridge University library, which has just about every volume of poetry and literature imaginable. I can roam at will there, and it is wonderful to have large quantities of world literature within walking distance of my home and workplace.

Some texts I choose not to set. I don't set poetry that is already complete in itself. The Shakespeare sonnets, for example, are beautiful to read but don't need music because they are perfect as they are. I also don't set poetry that has extremely dense imagery. The work of a religious poet like Gerard Manley Hopkins is, for me, impossible to set to music, although some have tried. John Donne is another metaphysical poet who is very difficult to set to music. While some composers have had success with his texts, I cannot compose to his words because when I read his poetry, I sense that the poems already have an internal music. In cases like these, instead of trying to solve the wrong problem it is generally better to find something else.

Another category that I have difficulty with is contemporary liturgical language. It is well-meaning but does not resonate for me in the same way that the King James Bible and the 1662 Book of Common Prayer do. Both were written in the golden age of the English language, and I find it very easy to set anything from either of those sources. They have a sense of reverence that calls forth the music in me. We live in an age where the liturgical language is functional, but it is not a language that lifts the soul to heaven.

A fair amount of the repertoire released on the Collegium label is Christmas music. For me, first and foremost, Christmas recalls happy memories of the way I celebrated as a child. Holiday festivities revolved around the family gatherings but also around my school chapel. Our Christmas carol service was the high point of the year, and we rehearsed for weeks to prepare for that event. In retrospect, I realize that our service was modeled after the King's College Cambridge Festival of Nine Lessons and Carols, an annual event which has inspired choirs all over the world.

From singing carols as a child in the choir, it seemed only a very short step to writing them. My early Christmas carols were among the first of my published works. I actually developed a love of Christmas music, along with the Christmas message, when I was a kid, and it has stayed with me ever since. At Christmas there's always the danger that something could go a bit wrong, whether it fails to snow on Christmas Day or the turkey is slightly burnt. But the music of Christmas is always perfect, so I love to remember and celebrate Christmas in music and song.

I think it is fair to say that my Christmas carols have become calling cards all over the world. If people know nothing else about me, they probably know that I wrote the *Shepherd's Pipe Carol*, the *Star Carol*, and some others. I went through a phase where I rebelled against that, thinking it was a bit of a millstone around my neck that made it difficult for people to take me seriously as a composer. I now have a more philosophical view, which is that I am fortunate to have written pieces which seem to have brought people pleasure over the years. They have made friends and a reputation for me all over the world. The Christmas carol is a humble art form that has a very long history—it is the earliest form of vernacular choral music, dating back to the Middle Ages. The carol has always brought me joy, and I think that has something to do with the magic of Christmas. The child in me always responds to Christmas, and the sense of wonder never seems to go away.

D. Views from the Composer to the Conductor Pertaining to Score Study and Preparation

In studying any score, the first thing I do is form a sound-picture of the music in my head: tempo, style, sonority, everything. I guess I don't need to do this when conducting my own music because I can already hear the ideal sound. But with mine or any other music, my business as conductor is to communicate that sound-picture to everybody else and close the gap between the perfect performance in my head and the real performance that I am hearing in front of me.

As the years go by, I think I am becoming slightly less of a perfectionist about matching my ideal performance to what I hear in reality. I have learned to give my performers some freedom to interpret the music how *they* hear it, while still guiding them toward my ideal sound. Twenty-five years ago I tended to be more insistent, saying things like the music must be performed with the quarter note equaling a metronome marking of 84 beats if that is what the composer indicated. These days I am more flexible and realize there is room for different performances in different circumstances, and I hope I am a better conductor because I have become less rigid.

Conductors always have to work under some sort of time constraint, because no one has unlimited rehearsal time. Other constraints include of the kind of occasion for which the conductor is selecting repertoire, as well as the acoustics of the hall. My job as a conductor is to take the performers, whether they are amateurs or professionals, as far as I can on a journey toward the best performance we can give. On the journey toward the perfect performance, all we can ever really hope for is to reach a point along that path of discovery, a stage along the road to a destination that does not really exist. What drives every musician is the quest to get as near to some kind of perfection as possible—preferably communicative perfection!

A three-cornered relationship exists between composer, performer, and audience, and if any one of those three is left out of the equation, the enterprise won't succeed. Conductors must bear in mind what the composer wants and how the audience will hear the performance. Composers must think of both the performers and the audience. It is like a three-legged stool—with only two legs, the stool falls down. The challenge of balancing this three-sided equation is immensely absorbing.

My first obligation as a conductor is to the composer. As a conductor, I believe that I am there to serve the composer, which is quite a responsibility. I feel most responsible to composers who are not present at the performance and have only me to advocate and represent their music. I hope I never give a performance that the composer would not appreciate.

The greater the music, the less likely the perfect performance becomes. You could perhaps give a perfect performance of a Viennese operetta like *Die Fledermaus*, but there is no such thing as a perfect performance of the Bach B Minor Mass. Most performances reveal one aspect or another, but it is like walking around a great cathedral—no matter where you stand, you never see all of it at once. There are so many facets to the Bach, that no matter how much you study it, some of it always remains hidden. I can return to the great works time and again because different things will "light up" and seem important; part of that journey along the road with no possible destination is that it continues to be rewarding to travel.

Probably all composers have been misinterpreted in one way or another. In some cases that may be because their notation is not precise enough. In pre-nineteenth century music, for example, many features of performance, such as tempo, dynamics, and ornamentation were only sketchily indicated. Notation itself has changed its meaning over the centuries, and voices, instruments, and pitch centers have changed too. Sometimes the notation is fine but conductors ignore simple things like metronome markings. The heartbeat of music is the pulse, and if the pulse is the wrong speed, it is very difficult for a performance to work. But what can you do?

Once a composition is published, it means what it says; it has been "made public." As public property, anybody can have at it and do what they want with it. If composers don't want that to happen, they should not publish their work. I used to get quite worked up if conductors did a piece of mine wrong. Now, I think I can be a bit more philosophical and say, "This particular performance was not the way I would have liked it to go, but the conductor might be seeing it in a way that is just as valid." Must be mellowing with age!

Conductors preparing to perform a piece must first study all the evidence, beginning with the printed score in the most trust-worthy available edition, and give this evidence the fairest possible trial. For example, composers include metronome markings because they want them to be observed—though admittedly they sometimes miscalculate. While Benjamin Britten was extremely accurate in his metronome markings, Herbert Howells once admitted to me that his markings were often wrong. As a conductor, I frequently wonder if Vaughan Williams really wanted his music as slow as he sometimes indicated. Other considerations include a review of significant recordings (you wouldn't conduct the *Chichester Psalms*, say, without checking the composer's own recordings), an understanding of the resources and occasions the composer wrote the music for, and a working grasp of historical performance practice (even twentieth-century music is historical now!). We must bear all those elements in mind when preparing each individual performance.

The final step is to add your personal interpretation to the music. Study of the score and of famous recordings alone may pro-duce a boring clone of someone else's performance. A conductor cannot skip the preparation—an uninformed performance will probably be a bad performance—but he or she must then *think* about and bring personal judgment to bear on the music. That doesn't mean plastering a spurious interpretation on top of the music; it means trying to draw out its meaning from within.

E. The Relationship Between the Composer and the Commissioning Party

Often the commission will define the structure of the piece. Frequently, the commissioning party will specify whether the piece should be *a cappella* or include an accompaniment or a particular instrumentation. Those musical decisions are sometimes taken out of my hands before I put one note on the paper. For example, my *Gloria* was to be performed by an eighty-voice choir in a hall with a rather dry acoustic. While this allowed me to write quite fast-moving and intricate passages without worrying that they would get swallowed up in the reverb, on the other hand, sustained *legato* passages proved to be more difficult. I knew what else was going to be programmed at the premiere concert, which left me with a clearly defined twenty minutes or so to fill in the program. I also knew the conductor only had a budget for ten to twelve instrumentalists. In that instance, the piece practically wrote itself.

Most of my music written before 1985 bears a dedication at the top of the first page. It was my practice to find out as much as I could about the commissioning organization. I would ask them to send me recordings of the group, and, if possible I would visit the performance hall to get a feel for the acoustics of the space. I crafted quite a number of pieces for a particular performance or occasion. What composers hope will happen is that if someone tells you what they are looking for in a piece, they are actually speaking for a lot of other groups too. Then your piece will have more than one performance in it, and others will want to use it as well. That was the case of the *Gloria*. Its length of just less than twenty minutes is suitable for several types of occasions, as is the text. The guidelines for that piece turned out to fit choirs the world over.

I tend to take the view that what I have written, I have written. I rarely alter anything once it is published. I do like to let a few months go by after the initial performance before putting a piece into print. When I return to a piece several months after its premiere, I can take another look at it and follow one of three options: 1) put it into print exactly as it stands, 2) put it into print with a few adjustments or changes, or 3) "bin" it. I have actually binned quite a few of my compositions, pieces I feel that, despite every best effort, did not turn out quite right. Rather than putting them into print, I would prefer that they be quietly forgotten. That is one of the advantages composers have over architects—most of our mistakes get buried. When an architect erects a bad building we all have to live with it because it is hard to hide.

With commissions, I like having the freedom to choose my own text. I enjoy searching for the right text to fit the occasion and have selected the texts for more than 90 percent of my pieces. On some occasions I have accepted an idea that someone else presented, such as *The Lord is my light and my salvation*, a psalm text that was brought to my attention by Ben Smith, the director of chapel music at Duke University. He said the text gave him great personal inspiration. I had never considered setting it to music, but when I looked at it, it did indeed speak to me. Most of the time, though, I prefer to choose my own material.

I stopped doing commissioned work in 1985 when I reached my fortieth birthday. Part of the reason for that was because I had been writing commissions almost exclusively for more than fifteen years. I felt I was on a treadmill and in real danger of repeating myself, because people tend to commission composers to write more of what they have written already. If you have done one festive and celebratory choral piece, then people say they want another one like that. I found myself getting into a bit of a rut and unable to break out into other areas of composition because I was not getting invited to write anything very different or challenging.

The other reason I got out of commissions is because I was not enjoying the deadlines. With all of the impending deadlines, I felt like I was becoming a bit of a slave to the calendar and sometimes even the clock. I needed some freedom to compose what I wanted when I wanted, and I have been working this way ever since. However, I still get asked to write pieces for the concerts that I conduct. For example, the Carnegie Hall concerts sponsored by Mid-America Productions have on three different occasions provided the opportunity to premiere my works with chorus and orchestra. I still respond to ideas and suggestions from the outside world, but in the end I do not take commissions in the sense of accepting a deadline and a sum of money. Many composers are very comfortable writing in that work pattern, but I needed to make a change. I perhaps write less now that I don't have as many deadlines, because, I have to admit, nothing focuses the mind of a composer like a deadline looming on the horizon, but I have been able to explore other areas of composition that were not possible before.

F. Views on the Teaching of Composition and How to Mentor the Young Composer

I taught composition for ten years, and in the late 1970s it was actually part of my job as music director at Clare College in

Cambridge. I soon discovered that as a composition teacher you cannot give composers inspiration or ideas, nor can you control the quality of a student's ideas. Talent is the mystery at the heart of all creative endeavors and was the subject of Peter Shaffer's play *Amadeus*. Why is it that Salieri, who did all of the right things by studying and "paying his dues," could only come up with mediocre ideas that in the end were for the most part forgettable? And how did Mozart, seemingly without trying, come up with marvelous ideas that the world remembers today? Nobody can teach that kind of gift.

Technique, however, is something that you *can* teach. I would emphasize the importance of first-class compositional technique in my teaching. The notes must do what you want them to do; students should not be struggling to express their ideas with an inadequate technique. There are some historical composers whose technical grounding did not match their inspiration. Francis Poulenc is a good example: he never studied at the Paris Conservatoire and was pretty much self-taught as a composer. This lack of training is particularly apparent in his large-scale structures (and the terrible voice-leading in his choral music!). His Organ Concerto consists of a string of striking ideas, but they are laid end-to-end with no real sense of connection.

In teaching composition, the best thing you can do is to first encourage students at the human level. Everybody deserves that. Then, create opportunities for composition students to hear their works performed; you will be doing them a great favor. In terms of what to teach, I would emphasize technique so that students are never held back from expressing themselves.

I first started by writing small pieces rather than attempting the "next great masterpiece," although I would not necessarily recommend this approach for everyone; sometimes you have to reach for the sky even if you fall short. While at Cambridge I had many stimulating discussions with Patrick Gowers, who felt I was being rather under-ambitious in the sort of music I was writing. He wanted me to be more adventurous and far-reaching in the scale of my works. It is funny—we did not see each other for almost twenty-five years, and when we met again, we resumed that same conversation. He asked me why I was not doing more!

All composers must find their own path. Some are called to be adventurers and explorers and write big epics from the time they are quite young, while others start small and work their way up to the bigger forms. I think I fall into the second category. I always admired those who tried great things, even if they did not quite succeed, but basically I am a musical magpie who collects sounds and ideas from anywhere and makes a nest from them.

I would advise young composers to take every opportunity to have their music performed. Even if it is not a very professional performance, you can learn a great deal just by hearing your work done. If you are serious about writing for choir, don't write just for choir, write for everything. Composition is composition. If you do not write well for instruments, then you probably will not write well for voices either. A professional composer should be able to write for any medium.

G. Individuals Who Were Especially Influential in My Development and Career

My parents were not musicians, but they were supportive and wise and gave me the best possible start in this profession. Perhaps because they did not know much about the music profession they did not know enough to warn me off it!

My director of music at Highgate School, Edward Chapman, was always encouraging. He made several suggestions about the direction I might go with my music and was the guiding force that led me to study at Cambridge, which turned out to be good advice. Chapman was a pupil of Charles Wood, who in turn was a pupil of Charles Villiers Stanford, a great composition teacher in the last years of the nineteenth century. I feel that I stand in a direct line of succession through Edward Chapman from Stanford, who studied in Germany at the time of Johannes Brahms. I believe they met.

Patrick Gowers gave me an important message in the 1960s, and that was, "Don't worry about serialism, twelve-tone composing. It is not for you. It may well fade. [It has.] Just be true to yourself." He had the sense to understand the kind of music I wanted to write. He had a firm academic grasp of good traditional writing—counterpoint and canons, fugues in the style of J. S. Bach, and orchestrating in the style of W. A. Mozart or Maurice Ravel. I must pay tribute to his fine teaching.

Sir David Willcocks helped me to make the big leap from aspiring composer to published composer. That was an amazing stroke of luck for a twenty-one-year-old. He helped me on the road to composing by creating performance opportunities for my music, and his willingness to comment on my manuscripts was always appreciated.

Clearly we have also all been taught by all of the great composers. This is not a frivolous remark because, in the end, every composer has to find his or her own way, but I learned the most from listening to the music and studying the scores of those who have gone before me. We all stand on the shoulders of our predecessors.

I return to some particular composers again and again because of the inspiration they have given me. Gregorian chant and Renaissance polyphony remain the golden threads running through almost all choral writing. I am hugely inspired by J. S. Bach and G. F. Handel, the twin peaks of the Baroque. Bach had the ability to combine head and heart in perfect equilibrium. W. A. Mozart and F. J. Haydn, of course, are also at the top of my tree. I enjoy the Romantics and have a particular soft spot for Maurice Ravel and Sergei Rachmaninoff. American composers, by which I mean the generation of Aaron Copland, Leonard Bernstein, and the Broadway songwriters, remain inspirational because of their integration of words and music: Jerome Kern, George Gershwin, Richard Rodgers, and later, Stephen Sondheim were influences on me.

The soil on which I grew up is also important . . . Ralph Vaughan Williams, Edward Elgar, Benjamin Britten, and especially William Walton have affected my compositional style. Walton's music is a wonderful combination of melancholy and huge physical excitement and energy. I met him in his last years. He was prodigiously gifted in his compositional and orchestral technique. While you might not particularly notice these influences when listening to my music, they have all been my inspirations.

I would also like to mention another British composer, Richard Rodney Bennett, because he is one of the composers who can do it all. He is both a concert and operatic composer with some very fine choral music. He is also active in the worlds of jazz and film music, and he does not seem to compromise any part of himself when he writes in this wide range of styles. He has shown my generation of composers the way.

The relationship with a publisher is like a Catholic marriage. Although I have branched out with Hinshaw Music (they publish much of my choral music in America), I have remained proudly associated with Oxford University Press for almost forty years. Oxford published Vaughan Williams in the days when there were no written contracts, only handshakes. Some of that old-fashioned, gentlemanly atmosphere remains today. I look upon Oxford and Hinshaw as members of my family that I simply could not be without.

H. Ten Works All Choral Conductors at All Levels Should Study

1. Any of the choral music of the Renaissance masters, particularly Tomas Luis da Victoria, is worth study. His music is an example of Renaissance polyphony at its finest.

2. The Monteverdi *Vespers* is uniquely representative of the music of the early seventeenth century.

3. J. S. Bach – both the *St. Matthew Passion* and the B Minor Mass.

4. George Frideric Handel – Every conductor should of course know *Messiah*, although among his oratorios *Saul*, *Solomon*, and *Israel in Egypt* are very fine.

5. Franz Joseph Haydn's *Creation* is an inspiration.

6. W. A. Mozart – I would like to recommend the C Minor Mass because everyone else will probably say the Requiem. The C Minor Mass is just as good.

7. The great Romantic Requiems: Hector Berlioz, Johannes Brahms, Giuseppe Verdi, and Gabriel Fauré. (That's cheating, I realize—four major works counted as one!)

8. In the twentieth century, the issue is whether to focus on big works with orchestra or smaller, *a cappella* works. I adore the *Chichester Psalms* by Leonard Bernstein; they are a

masterpiece of their kind, but life wouldn't be the same without the Igor Stravinsky *Symphony of Psalms* and the Maurice Duruflé Requiem.

9. To represent English music, I can't decide between Herbert Howells's *Hymnus Paradisi* and William Walton's *Belshazzar's Feast*.

10. György Ligeti's *Lux aeterna* is unlike any other piece that I have mentioned.

11. While this exceeds my allotment of ten pieces, I would be remiss if I did not mention the Benjamin Britten *War Requiem*.

I. The Future of Choral Music

The standards for choral music have risen enormously. Audiences can expect the best choirs to have the same expertise, accuracy, and artistry as orchestras, and that absolutely was not the case forty years ago. I can remember attending concerts in London in my teens, and although I knew rather little about performance, I recognized that on many occasions the orchestra was in tune and in time but the choir was flat and behind the beat. The obvious answer was that the orchestra was professional and the choir was amateur. Nevertheless, something like that would not happen with the leading choirs today. Our expectations (created in part by the wealth of fine choral CDs now readily available) are higher, so the standards continue to rise.

The emergence of professional choirs has been exciting for us in Britain. I use the term "professional" to refer not just to professional leadership, but to the singers actually earning a full-time living from choral singing . . . choirs like the Monteverdi Choir, Polyphony, the Gabrieli Consort, the Sixteen, and, indeed, my own group, the Cambridge Singers. These choirs are mostly chamber sized because practical economics limit the membership to thirty or so voices. The recordings made by these groups have opened people's ears to what a choir can do. And, I would say, the best of our cathedral and collegiate choirs have never been better.

If there is a down side to the development of professional choirs, it is similar to the down side of professional sports. Because we now have professionals, many talented amateurs are no longer active participants, only consumers. Rather than singing in a choir themselves, they pay others to do it for them while they listen to recordings and attend concerts. People now attend *Messiah* concerts given by professional choirs instead of singing in their own performance of that work, which would have been inconceivable thirty years ago. The danger of just consuming professional performances is that we forget the joy that comes from participating in choral music.

It is more important than ever that children learn and discover singing for themselves. Music is not just something you listen to—it is something you do! Music is like swimming, and most of us would agree that every kid should try swimming to find out whether he or she enjoys it.

In Britain a majority of schools have almost eliminated singing altogether. Students are leaving high school without ever having sung in a choir at any time in their education. This is a worrisome trend that must be reversed. If we have a generation of parents coming along that have never sung, they will probably not teach their children to sing; then singing will become the province of a select few professionals without any support from a thriving amateur sector of music makers.

I believe that singing is a natural activity everybody should experience. We are always at risk of losing music in our schools because there are those who will say there is no time for choir when literacy and numeracy have to be taught. But when singing and music get squeezed out, something central to education and to ourselves and the chance to experience great music and engage in a natural and wonderful activity are lost. Singing is an expression of our deepest selves, and this is the way our souls find a voice through our bodies. We lose it at our peril.

J. Comprehensive List of Works for Choir

(Note: asterisked items are published by Hinshaw Music, Inc., in the USA.)

Anthems for Mixed Voices:

A Choral Amen, SSAATTBB unaccompanied, Oxford University Press

*A Choral Fanfare, SATB unaccompanied, Oxford University Press

*A Clare Benediction, SATB unaccompanied or with keyboard or orchestra, Oxford University Press

A Crown of Glory, SATB and organ, Oxford University Press

*A Gaelic Blessing, SATB and organ or organ and guitar, RSCM Publications

*A Prayer of Saint Patrick, SATB unaccompanied, Oxford University Press

All Creatures of Our God and King, mixed choir, brass ensemble, timpani, percussion, organ or mixed choir and orchestra, Oxford University Press

*All Things Bright and Beautiful, SATB or unison voices with piano or orchestra, Oxford University Press

Arise, Shine, SATB and organ, Oxford University Press

*As the Bridegroom to His Chosen, SATB and organ or harp and strings, Oxford University Press

Be Thou My Vision, SATB, with piano or organ or orchestra, Oxford University Press

Beautiful River (*Shall We Gather by the River*), SATB, Bourne Music Company

Behold, the Tabernacle of God, SATB and organ or orchestra, Oxford University Press

Cantate Domino, SATB unaccompanied, Oxford University Press

Cantus, mixed choir (with optional solo soprano) and organ or brass ensemble, Oxford University Press

Christ the Lord Is Risen Again, SATB and organ or orchestra, Oxford University Press

Come Down, O Love Divine, unaccompanied double SATB choir, Oxford University Press

For the Beauty of the Earth, SATB and piano or orchestra, Oxford University Press

Gloria in excelsis Deo (from *Gloria*), SATB accompanied by full orchestra or brass, percussion, and organ, Oxford University Press

Go Forth into the World in Peace, SATB and organ or strings, Oxford University Press

God Be in My Head, SATB unaccompanied, Oxford University Press

How Firm a Foundation, SATB and organ, with congregation (optional), Oxford University Press

Hymn to the Creator of Light, double SATB choir unaccompanied, Oxford University Press

I Believe in Springtime, unison with optional mixed voices, and piano or orchestra, Oxford University Press

I Will Lift up Mine Eyes, SATB and organ or orchestra, Oxford University Press

I Will Sing with the Spirit, SATB with organ, Oxford University Press

I Will Worship the Lord (*Call to Worship*), SATB and keyboard, Oxford University Press

Let Us Go in Peace, SATB and piano, Hinshaw Music, Inc.

Look at the World, unison children's and/or SATB choir with piano or organ or orchestral accompaniment, Oxford University Press

Lord of the Dance (arr. Rutter), SATB with descant or unison with descant, Stainer & Bell (Hope Publishing in USA)

Loving Shepherd of Thy Sheep, SATB unaccompanied (with soprano solo), Oxford University Press

Now Thank We All Our God, mixed choir, brass ensemble, timpani, percussion and organ, Oxford University Press

O Be Joyful in the Lord, SATB and organ or orchestra, Oxford University Press

O Clap Your Hands, SATB and organ or orchestra, Oxford University Press

Open Thou Mine Eyes, SATB unaccompanied, Oxford University Press

Pie Jesu, soprano solo, SATB choir and organ, Oxford University Press

Praise the Lord, O My Soul, SATB and organ or ensemble (three trumpets, two trombones, timpani, and organ), Oxford University Press

Praise Ye the Lord, SATB (with baritone soloist or semi-chorus) and organ or orchestra, Oxford University Press

Psalm 150, SATB choir and SSS soli or semi-chorus, with organ or brass ensemble, timpani, percussion, and organ (also available with accompaniment for full orchestra), Oxford University Press (Collegium Music Publications in USA)

The Lord Bless You and Keep You, SATB with organ or strings, Oxford University Press

The Lord Is My Light and My Salvation, SATB, clarinet and organ or clarinet, harp, and strings, Oxford University Press

The Lord Is My Shepherd, SATB and organ or small orchestra (oboe, harp, strings), Oxford University Press

The Peace of God, SATB and organ, Oxford University Press

Thy Perfect Love, SATB and organ or strings, Oxford University Press

Veni sancte spiritus, mixed choir with organ, Oxford University Press

*Wedding Canticle (Blessed Are All They That Fear the Lord), SATB, flute
and guitar or piano, Oxford University Press

*When the Saints Go Marching In, SATB with keyboard, Oxford
University Press

*Wings of the Morning, SATB choir and piano or chamber orchestra,
Oxford University Press

Part-songs for Mixed Voices:

*Banquet Fugue, SATB and piano or combo, Oxford University Press

Black Sheep, SATB unaccompanied, Oxford University Press

Blow, Blow Thou Winter Wind, SSATB and piano or small orchestra,
Oxford University Press

Canticles of America, SATB, Bourne Music Company

Down by the Riverside, SATB and piano or orchestra, Oxford University
Press

Draw on, Sweet Night, SATB unaccompanied, Oxford University Press

*Fiddler Man, SATB and piano, Oxford University Press

Five Traditional Songs, SATB unaccompanied voices, Oxford University
Press

Good Ale, SATB and keyboard, Oxford University Press

*Home Is a Special Kind of Feeling (Finale from The Wind in the Willows),
SATB, Oxford University Press

It Was a Lover and His Lass, SATB unaccompanied, Oxford University
Press

*Let's Begin Again (Finale from The Reluctant Dragon), Oxford
University Press

*Musica Dei Donum, mixed choir and solo flute, Oxford University Press

My True Love Hath My Heart, SATB unaccompanied, Oxford University
Press

Nice Young Maidens, SATB unaccompanied, Oxford University Press

O Waly, Waly, mixed voices, Oxford University Press

Riddle Song, SATB and piano or orchestra, Oxford University Press

Rocking, SATB and keyboard, Carl Fischer Music

Seeds Grow to Plants, SATB and keyboard, Bourne Music Company

*Soldier Boy, SATB and piano, Oxford University Press

The British Grenadiers, SATB, Oxford University Press

The Heavenly Aeroplane, two-part upper voices or SATB choir with
either piano, drums (optional), and double bass/bass guitar or
orchestra, Oxford University Press

*The Terrible Tale of Tom Gilligan, SATB and piano, Oxford University
Press

*Three American Lyrics (Fiddler Man, Soldier Boy, The Terrible Tale of
Tom Gilligan), SATB and piano, Oxford University Press

Two American Folk Songs, SATB unaccompanied, Oxford University
Press

Two Songs from Five Childhood Lyrics, SATB unaccompanied, Oxford
University Press

When Daisies Pied, SATB unaccompanied, Oxford University Press

Anthems for Upper Voices:

*A Clare Benediction, unison (or two-part) with keyboard or orchestra,
Oxford University Press

*All Things Bright and Beautiful, unison (with optional second part)
voices with piano or orchestra, Oxford University Press

*For the Beauty of the Earth, SS or SA and piano or orchestra, Oxford
University Press

God Be in My Head, SSA choir unaccompanied, Oxford University
Press

*I Will Sing With the Spirit, two-part upper voices and piano, Oxford
University Press

*Look at the World, unison children's choir, piano or organ or orchestral
accompaniment, Oxford University Press

Rocking, SSA and keyboard, Carl Fischer Music

*The Lord Bless You and Keep You, SA with piano accompaniment,
Oxford University Press

*The Peace of God, SSA and organ, Oxford University Press

Carols for Choir:

A *Merry Christmas* (arrangement), SA unaccompanied, Oxford
University Press

A *Virgin Most Pure* (arrangement), SSA and soloist or semi-chorus
and piano or organ, Oxford University Press

Angel Tidings (arrangement), SSATB and piano or orchestra, Oxford
University Press

*Angels' Carol, SATB and harp or piano or orchestra (also a version
for SA), Oxford University Press

Away in a Manger (arrangement), SATB and piano or orchestra,
Oxford University Press

*Candlelight Carol, SATB and organ (also available for SSAA),
Oxford University Press

Child in a Manger (arrangement), SATB voices with piano or organ or
orchestra, Oxford University Press

*Christmas Lullaby, SATB and organ or piano or small orchestra
(also available for SSAA), Oxford University Press

Christmas Night (arrangement), SATB and piano or organ or strings,
Oxford University Press

Cradle Song (arr.), SATB unaccompanied with optional solo (or unison semi-chorus), Oxford University Press

*Deck the Hall (arr.), SATB unaccompanied (also available SSAA
unaccompanied), Oxford University Press

Donkey Carol, SATB and piano or orchestra or brass (also available
SA and piano or orchestra or brass), Oxford University Press

*Dormi, Jesu, for mixed choir and organ or strings, Oxford University
Press

Down in Yon Forest (arr.), baritone soloist, SATB, and piano or
orchestra, Oxford University Press

Flemish Carol (arr.), SATB and piano or orchestra, Oxford University
Press

Gabriel's Message (arr.), SATB and piano or orchestra (also available
SSAA unaccompanied), Oxford University Press

*Go Tell It on the Mountain (arr.), SATB and piano or orchestra, Oxford University Press

Here We Come a-Wassailing (arr.), SATB and piano or orchestra or brass ensemble, Oxford University Press

I Saw Three Ships (arr.), SATB and piano or orchestra or brass ensemble, Oxford University Press

*I Wonder as I Wander (arr.), SATB unaccompanied, Oxford University Press

Il est né le divin enfant (arr.), SATB and piano or orchestra (also available for SSA and instrumental accompaniment), Oxford University Press

In dulci jubilo (arr.), SATB and piano or orchestra (also available SSA unaccompanied), Oxford University Press

Infant Holy, Infant Lowly, SATB, piano (also available SSA and keyboard), Carl Fischer Music

Jesus Child, SATB and piano or orchestra or brass ensemble, Oxford University Press

*Joy to the World! (arr.), SATB and organ or orchestra, Oxford University Press

King Jesus Hath a Garden (arr.), SATB and piano or flute, harp, and strings (also available SSA unaccompanied), Oxford University Press

Love Came Down at Christmas, SATB and piano or organ or strings, Oxford University Press

Lute-Book Lullaby (arr.), SSAA voices, unaccompanied, Oxford University Press

Mary's Lullaby, SATB and piano or flute, oboe, harp, and strings (also available for SSA), Oxford University Press

Nativity Carol, SSA or SATB and piano or strings, Oxford University Press

Noel nouvelet (arr.), SATB and piano or orchestra, Oxford University Press

O Come, O Come, Immanuel (arr.), SATB and piano or organ or small orchestra, Oxford University Press

*_O Holy Night_ (Adolphe Adam), SATB and organ or orchestra, Oxford University Press

*_O Tannenbaum_ (arr.), SATB unaccompanied, Oxford University Press

Of a Rose, a Lovely Rose, SATB and piano or orchestra, Oxford University Press

Of the Father's Love Begotten (arr.), SATB and piano or organ, strings and organ (optional), Oxford University Press

Past Three a Clock (arr.), semi-chorus or soloist, SATB, and piano or orchestra (also available SSA, unaccompanied), Oxford University Press

Personent hodie (arr.), SATB choir and keyboard or small ensemble (also available SSA and harp or piano), Oxford University Press

Quelle est cette odeur agréable? (arr.), SATB and piano or orchestra, Oxford University Press

Quem pastores laudavere (arr.), SATB unaccompanied (also available SSA unaccompanied), Oxford University Press

Quittez, pasteurs (arr.), SATB and semi-chorus, piano or orchestra, Oxford University Press

*_Rejoice and Be Merry_, SATB choir and brass ensemble with (optional) organ and (optional) handbells, Oxford University Press

*_Rise Up, Shepherd, and Follow_ (arr.), solo baritone and SATB chorus, unaccompanied, Oxford University Press

Sans Day Carol (arr.), SATB and piano or orchestra, Oxford University Press

Shepherd's Noel (arr.), SATB and piano or orchestra, Oxford University Press

Shepherd's Pipe Carol, SATB and piano or orchestra (also available SSA and piano or orchestra), Oxford University Press

Sing We to This Merry Company, SATB and organ or orchestra or brass ensemble, Oxford University Press

Somerset Wassail (arr.), SATBB unaccompanied, Oxford University Press

Star Carol, SATB and piano or orchestra, with optional children's chorus, Oxford University Press

Stille Nacht (arr.), SATB and piano or small orchestra (also available SA with SSA semi-chorus and guitar or piano), Oxford University Press

The Coming of Our King (arr.), SATB and piano or orchestra, Oxford University Press

The Holly and the Ivy (arr.), SATB and piano or instrumental ensemble, Oxford University Press

The Infant King (arr.), SATB and piano or orchestra (also available SSA unaccompanied), Oxford University Press

The Linden Tree Carol (arr.), two solo voices and SSAA choir unaccompanied, Oxford University Press

The Twelve Days of Christmas (arr.), SATB and piano or orchestra or brass ensemble, Oxford University Press

The Very Best Time of Year, SATB and piano or orchestra, Oxford University Press

The Wild Wood Carol, SATB choir and baritone solo with piano or orchestra, Oxford University Press

There Is a Flower, SATB unaccompanied, Oxford University Press

Three Kings of Orient (arr.), SATB and piano or orchestra, Oxford University Press

Tomorrow Shall Be My Dancing Day (arr.), SSA, and harp or piano, Oxford University Press

We Wish You a Merry Christmas (arr.), SATB and piano or orchestra, Oxford University Press

Wexford Carol (arr.), SATB and optional baritone solo, Oxford University Press

What Sweeter Music, SATB and organ or string orchestra, Oxford University Press

Zion Hears the Watchmen's Voices (from Cantata No. 140), J. S. Bach,
  ed. John Rutter, unison (with SATB in concluding chorale),
  strings and continuo with optional instruments (two oboes,
  clarinet, bassoon) in concluding chorale

Carols for Unison Voices:

*Carol of the Children, unison voices (with optional second part) and
  piano or orchestra, Oxford University Press
Coventry Carol, unison voices with an accompaniment played on a
  keyboard instrument or sung by an SSA semi-chorus, Oxford
  University Press
Donkey Carol, arr. by Pont, Oxford University Press
Jesus Child, unison voices with a simplified accompaniment for piano,
  Oxford University Press
Nativity Carol, unison voices with a simplified piano accompaniment,
  Oxford University Press
Shepherd's Pipe Carol, unison with optional descant and piano or orches-
  tra, Oxford University Press
Star Carol, unison voices with a simplified piano accompaniment,
  Oxford University Press
Three Carols (A Merry Christmas, In dulci jubilo, The Holly and the
  Ivy; arr.), SS and SSA unaccompanied, Oxford University Press

Larger Choral Works:

Birthday Madrigals, mixed choir with optional double bass and
  optional piano, Oxford University Press
*Brother Heinrich's Christmas, a fable with music for narrator and
  mixed choir with small orchestra or oboe, bassoon, and piano,
  Oxford University Press
Fancies, SATB choir and piano or small orchestra, Oxford
  University Press
Five Childhood Lyrics, SATB unaccompanied mixed voices (with some
  divisi), Oxford University Press

Gloria, mixed voices, brass, percussion, and organ, Oxford
  University Press

Magnificat, soprano or mezzo-soprano solo, SATB chorus and either
  orchestra or chamber ensemble and organ, Oxford University
  Press

Mass of the Children, soprano and baritone soli, children's choir,
  mixed choir, and orchestra or chamber ensemble, Oxford
  University Press

Psalm 150, SATB choir and SSS soli or semi-chorus with organ or
  brass ensemble, timpani, percussion, and organ, Oxford
  University Press (Collegium Music Publications in USA)

Psalmfest, soprano and tenor soloists and SATB choir with keyboard
  or chamber ensemble or orchestra, Oxford University Press

Requiem, soprano soloist, mixed choir, and small orchestra or chamber ensemble, Oxford University Press

Te Deum, SATB and organ or brass or orchestra, Oxford University
  Press

The Falcon, SATB chorus (with semi-chorus), boys' choir (optional),
  and orchestra, Oxford University Press

The Reluctant Dragon, narrator, soloists, mixed chorus, and
  instrumental ensemble (strings, percussion, and two keyboard
  instruments) or piano, Oxford University Press

The Sprig of Thyme, mixed choir with piano or chamber ensemble
  (using one player per string part) or chamber orchestra, Oxford
  University Press

The Wind in the Willows, five soloists, narrator, SATB chorus, and
  instrumental ensemble, Oxford University Press

When Icicles Hang, SATB (with tenor solo) and small orchestra,
  Oxford University Press

Part-songs for Upper Voices:

It Was a Lover and His Lass, SA (with divisi) and piano, Oxford
  University Press

My True Love Hath My Heart, SSAA, Oxford University Press

Three Folk-Songs from *The Spring of Thyme*, unison voices and piano or ensemble, Oxford University Press

When Daisies Pied, SSAA and piano, Oxford University Press

Part-songs for Men's Voices:

Two Folk-songs for Male Voices from *The Sprig of Thyme*, TBB, Oxford University Press

Collections:

100 Carols for Choirs, edited and arranged by David Willcocks and John Rutter, Oxford University Press

Carols for Choirs 2, edited and arranged by David Willcocks and John Rutter, Oxford University Press

Carols for Choirs 3, edited and arranged by David Willcocks and John Rutter, Oxford University Press

Carols for Choirs 4, SA voices, edited and arranged by David Willcocks and John Rutter, Oxford University Press

Eight Christmas Carols, mixed voices and piano, Oxford University Press

Five Traditional Songs, SATB unaccompanied, Oxford University Press

Folk-Songs for Choirs 1, edited by John Rutter, mixed voices, Oxford University Press

Folk-Songs for Choirs 2, edited by John Rutter, mixed voices, Oxford University Press

*John Rutter Anthems (a collection of eleven pieces), SATB and piano, Oxford University Press

The Sprig of Thyme, mixed choir with piano or chamber ensemble, Oxford University Press

Twelve Christmas Carols, mixed voices and small orchestra or piano, Oxford University Press

chapter **8**

z. randall **Stroope**

A. Biography

Z. Randall Stroope (b. 1953) is widely known as a conductor, lecturer, and composer. He is the artistic director of a summer music festival in England and frequently conducts in Carnegie Hall, Lincoln Center, Washington National Cathedral, and other well-known venues in the United States.

Stroope conducted choral and orchestral concerts in Vienna and Salzburg as part of those cities' 250th celebration of Mozart's birth. He has also guest conducted in Singapore, Lithuania, and Canada.

Choral groups under his direction have taken thirty-five national tours and fifteen international tours, including trips to Italy, China, Japan, Russia, Sweden, the Baltics, Finland, central Europe, England, Canada, and South Africa. He is sought after as a lecturer and guest conductor. Stroope has headlined summer ACDA conventions in many states and has conducted twenty-five all-state choirs. Stroope led his performers at the ACDA National Convention, numerous regional ACDA conventions, and at the meeting of the International Society of Music Education in Pretoria, South Africa.

Stroope studied composition with Cecil Effinger and Normand Lockwood, both students of Nadia Boulanger (who was a student of Gabriel Fauré) and has sold more than a million and a half copies of music. He was the ACDA Raymond Brock commissioned composer for 2004, and his commission "We Beheld Once Again the Stars" was performed at all of the ACDA Regional Conventions. Of his thirteen recorded compact discs, three are of his own music, *Passages I, I & III: The Choral Music of Z. Randall Stroope.*

Stroope is director of choral activities at the prestigious Rowan University in Glassboro, New Jersey, where he is director of choral studies. His wife, Cheryl, is a middle school choral music teacher in the area.

***

My father sang tenor; he could read shape notes and often directed music when I was growing up at a little Baptist church near our home in southern New Mexico. He wrote poetry and was a man of great intellect, even though he was orphaned at age two and had only an eighth-grade education. My mother was a wonderful improviser at the piano—she could play anything she heard. I grew up hearing the piano constantly. I started studying piano at age eight and became a church accompanist at age twelve. My mother was also a Southwest landscape painter who was quite gifted for having very little formal education. The kitchen table always had paint on it.

From my parents, I learned the value of reading poetry and music, being creative, and developing an awareness of color. We lived on a farm-style ranch, so I grew up in an agricultural, country environment. That pastoral life gave me time to contemplate and develop a comfort for being alone. As a composer, you are partnered with yourself and your thoughts a great deal of the time. To this day, I fondly reflect on those rural life experiences and value quiet time.

When I was in middle school, my parents sent me to a summer school in Dallas that taught basic harmony, improvisation, group singing, and fundamental counterpoint. By the time I got to high school, I already had some training in writing and performing music at a higher level.

When I started thinking about a career, I initially considered history. I love history and had some wonderful models in that field, but encouragement from my high school choral director, Carol Brashear, provided a springboard for my eventual study of music instead.

The high school choir of which I was a member performed "Sure on this Shining Night" by Samuel Barber. I was so taken by the wonderful words of James Agee that I can remember turning to someone else in the choir and telling them that someday I would set that poem to music. And I did—albeit twenty-five years later! I can't say that my setting "holds a candle" (as my father used to say) to the Barber rendition, but that was not my goal.

Then came university training, where I received a bachelor of music education (voice and piano), a master of music (voice performance), and a doctorate in conducting. The focus of these degrees varied, but each was an important "piece of the pie" in creating a well-rounded education.

B. The Creative Process

My inspiration for writing music comes primarily from two sources—text and strong inner belief. A composer must relate to the text in order for the inner creative process to have any chance at all of synthesizing it into a musical context. For me, every text is a new discovery. Not knowing which way the composition will take me or how long it will take to get there is sort of like leaving on a vacation without any idea of a travel route or a destination. My faith is what I feel is the "spark" that ignites my thought and creative energy.

To describe my compositional process as "typical" would be inaccurate. Some of the most difficult pieces mechanically, those with the greatest complexity of parts and instrumental accompaniment, frequently take the least amount of time for me to put on the page. In contrast, a four-part motet of economical design can often be the most problematic. My composition teacher, Normand Lockwood, once told me, "You must always write with the essence in mind. It is easy to write with a lot of notes. But it takes a master to say the same thing with only a few notes, where every note counts." He was always challenging me to find the essence of a chord, not to dance around and obscure it with games of complication. And to do *that* takes time.

My compositional regimen includes writing every day. Just as athletes have to work out every day to stay in shape, a composer needs to cultivate creativity on a consistent basis. Creativity is not a spigot that can be turned on and off.

When writing vocal or instrumental music, I use the same philosophical approach to the creative process with the same musical language, per se, but the "catalyst that inspires the muse" is somewhat different. The text should, of course, have a strong influence on the outcome of the creative process in choral works, while music written for instruments is guided more by the composer's concept and emotions. Some works are strongly programmatic, like the Dukas *Sorcerer's Apprentice*, while others are more general and guided by the composer's palette.

In the end, I trust that the most influential composers are not "choral composers" or "orchestral composers" but *composers*. I think the art of composition synthesizes dramatic, visual, auditory, and all manners of human experience and that a dose of all of these elements and more exists in every composition, no matter the medium.

C. The Relationship Between Text and Music

The relationship between text and music defies a finite explanation. Perhaps this is because the "human variable" is so great an influence. The way a particular human being relates or responds to a poem, for instance, is different in many ways from any other person's perception. And, if that person sets the poem to music, then those unique skills, perceptions, and emotions take equally unique journeys on the printed page.

On the flip side, human beings share basic needs, wants, and emotions. We *all* have these in varying amounts. So therein lies the difficulty in explaining relationships between text and music—there is as much uniqueness as there is commonality. Some compositions seem to relate to many people in many lands, while other works tend to find little audience. I believe that the listener of music—certainly choral music—has a window into the composer's soul. And somehow, in peering through that window, audiences better understand their *own* souls. A composer's success is really not based on *how he or she relates to the listener*, but how the *listener relates to and better understands himself* after listening to the composer's music. The music connects the emotional circuitry inside the audience member, and he or she feels like things make sense when certain music is played.

As to authors, there are several for whom I have a strong affinity—Emily Dickinson, Sarah Teasdale, Christina Rossetti, Robert Frost, James Agee, and others—because they seem to speak a language to which I relate. Over the years, I have used the poetry of almost 150 different authors for my compositions, and although I have set several Teasdale poems (perhaps my favorite poet), I have no desire to set her entire output to music. In many ways, the drama and people's struggle to overcome seemingly insurmountable obstacles inspires me.

D. Views from the Composer to the Conductor Pertaining to Score Study and Preparation

The conductors who seem to have the most success are those who think in terms of the duality of being a servant to the music itself while giving way to their own creative imprint at the same time. Many musical pillars should not be varied, while others are more flexible. Tempo markings are often the source of greatest violation—there are certainly some obvious influential factors, not the least of which is the acoustic, but gross variance from the indicated tempo raises serious questions about judgment. Other elements, however, particularly in the area of expression, allow for more individual flexibility.

Score study is one of the most important tasks of the conductor. It is also a task that is easily shortchanged when the myriad of daily responsibilities descend on the conductor. Conductors who set aside regularly scheduled daily time for score study have more investment and understanding in the process of music making, and the results often bear that out as well.

E. The Relationship Between the Composer and the Commissioning Party

Many of the greatest works in the choral repertoire have developed out of the commissioning process. Randall Thompson's "Alleluia" comes to mind. (This piece was commissioned for the opening exercises of the new Berkshire Music Center at Tanglewood). Creativity works best within clear but flexible parameters, such as general voicing, instrumental possibilities, the level of the performing ensemble, and so on. In my view the best commissioning agreement leaves a lot of latitude for the composer to exercise an utmost measure of creativity—like flying on an airline to a loosely agreed destination—you get plenty of elbowroom, have as much time as you want to get there, and your seatbelt doesn't always have to be locked and "snug around your waist." In other words, you can move around and enjoy the trip.

I normally choose the text, as I find it very difficult to write a piece using words chosen for me—they may or may not relate to my creative psyche. It is also important that composers try to feature some aspect of their craft that also highlights the ability of the ensemble. If I were writing music to be choreographed by an Olympic ice skater, the score might include a juxtaposition of quiet, gentle moments against angular, brilliantly colorful passages. I recently wrote "Ode to Joy" for the Texas All-State Choir, knowing they have the ability to tackle anything. Accordingly, I wrote a difficult piece with full sonorities, a wide range of color, and all sorts of compositional devices that seemed appropriate for an ensemble with great facility. *Knowing* the ability of the ensemble and *writing* for that ability are major keys to success.

Whether or not it is stated in the commission agreement, most commissioning parties expect (or desire at the very least) for the finished work to be published at some point. Ensembles

195

want their "influence" on choral repertoire to be noted by the publication of the commission. This is entirely logical and understandable. Composers should weigh the actual decision to publish a commission or not over an ample time period. My teacher Normand Lockwood published very little, though he was a consummate master. Part of the creative process is the waiting period after the performance of a piece. That waiting process is the time when a piece is "cooking." After you put all of the ingredients in and it looks great, you have to let it cook or gestate for a while. A composition has to have some time on the road before publishing is even considered. "Waiting" is an art that is neither liked nor practiced enough.

F. Views on Teaching Composition and How to Mentor the Young Composer

My list of tenets as a composer includes:

1. Be well versed in the art of counterpoint and harmony. There is no substitute for studying the craft.

2. Find a composer with whom you identify and whose writing you respect. Contact him or her, and ask to meet personally at some mutually convenient time to look at some of your recent works. This can be very stimulating and motivating. (I cold called Jean Berger, a wonderful and highly skilled composer, many years ago, and he simply said, "No."—he could be a little abrupt. But then he followed that with one of the most important statements in my compositional career: "You need to study with Normand Lockwood—he is the master. I go to Normand when I have questions." And so I called "Mr. Lockwood," and we met together for the

next two decades! Normand Lockwood studied with Nadia Boulanger, who, in turn, studied with Gabriel Fauré.) The mentoring process is vital. Take advantage of it!

3. Be a student, not a pillager, of the choral art. Be a learner all of your life. Do not use the choral art as a springboard to promote your career. Promote choral music instead.

4. Be more concerned with quality than quantity. *Publish only one out of every four pieces you write.* Even the great master composers of the ages wrote "flops." (Handel wrote lots of them.) Quality craftsmanship and the desire to make a difference should be the motivation in writing, not financial gain.

   When I was in college, I tuned pianos on Saturdays at a factory/warehouse that made and sold lots of pianos. I worked back in a dingy room with many pianos (and piano parts) strewn about and would tune all day with occasional "checks" by a master piano tuner who oversaw my work. Eventually, because I knew it paid more money, I asked if I might go out and tune "professionally" in privates homes and such, and his response was, "When you have tuned one thousand pianos, you will be ready to be on your own." For the same reason, it is important for young composers to write, write, and write some more. The goal should be to become a wonderful composer who has something different and sincere to say. In time, publishing may very well grow out of that creative output.

5. Lastly, my credo: Free your mind from the narrow con-straints of conformity. Keep your ego in check, and allow students to teach you as much as you teach them. Enjoy spending your life wandering through the halls of creativity.

G. Individuals Who Were Especially Influential in My Development and Career

There is a phrase taped above my desk that reads, "We become like those with whom we spend our time." I have lead a fairytale life in many ways, being at the right place at the right time, and have worked with some of the finest people ever created. The first wonderful influence in my life was my mother, Mary Ellen Stroope. In addition to being a great parent, she was the person who first taught me to improvise at the piano. Improvisation, to my mother, was like drinking water or breathing. As a result, I frequently sit down at the piano to this day and just improvise for a half hour or so. Improvising is a wonderful release, and I am indebted to my mother for recognizing its importance.

Another early influence was my college piano teacher, Andrzej Wasowski, a Polish pianist who, at the time, was one of the world's leading interpreters of the music of Frédéric Chopin (and he also gave a new meaning to the phrase "artistic temperament"). He taught me to think and play musically and to revel in all of the aspects that define musicality. He didn't publish books on it, he didn't talk about it, he *lived* it. "Don't go on to the second note unless the first one is musical." "Let one note excite the next." He had a "love affair" with sound, and his artistry could make you weep at a moment's notice. Very little was said in piano lessons with him. But volumes of understanding took place.

I went to the University of Colorado for graduate school and received a master's degree in vocal performance. While there, I studied with John Paton, a wonderful performer and language expert. He made me aware of the sound and color of language. The well-known vocal pedagogue Berton Coffin taught me vocal pedagogy and the tenets of vocal sonority, which have been immensely helpful in conducting and writing.

Later on, George Umberson, the former director of the School of Music at Arizona State University, taught me intolerance for mediocrity and artificiality. He was raised in the Southwest, where people are generally "straight shooters," and he had little patience for those who substituted artificial for "real." There can be a lot of facade and artificiality in the arts world, and he helped me appreciate (and seek) people who are sincere and without pretense.

In my post-college years, I studied privately with Cecil Effinger and Normand Lockwood. I studied for about two years with Effinger (an oboist and composer) and for about twenty years with Normand Lockwood. Lockwood embodied the consummate artist—he even looked like a composer with his tweed sweater, messy work table, and, of course, the pipe. He and his wife, Vona, took me in and treated me like a grandson. We had afternoon tea together, we shared family stories, and we even picked weeds out of their garden on occasion. I learned from them that to be a great artist you first have to be a great human being. They were both.

Probably the last major influence was Margaret Hillis. "Ms. Hillis" was the last person with whom I studied conducting. I would fly to Chicago once a month and spend two mornings with her, mostly looking at choral/orchestral works. She taught me about conducting, score marking, the choral/orchestral repertoire, and a more professional manner in which to approach music. I will be forever indebted to her for her gift of craftsmanship.

H. Ten Works All Choral Conductors at All Levels Should Study

These are ten pieces that, in my view, all choral conductors should study:

1. "Sicut cervus" by Giovanni Pierluigi da Palestrina
2. "Ave verum corpus" by William Byrd
3. *Messiah* by George Frideric Handel
4. *Cantata No. 4* by Johann Sebastian Bach
5. *Lord Nelson Mass* by F. J. Haydn
6. "Ave verum" by W. A. Mozart
7. "Wie lieblich sind deine Wohnungen" (*Requiem*) by Johannes Brahms
8. *Requiem* by Maurice Duruflé
9. "Come to Me, My Love" by Norman Dello Joio
10. *Reincarnations* by Samuel Barber

These are masterful works by masterful composers and are excellent mediums for teaching tone, style, articulation, color, note grouping, language, harmonic structure, and all manner of musicality. No list cures all ills, but this one is a healthy start.

I. The Future of Choral Music

Several trends, musical and non-musical, have made (and are making) a major impact on choral music. As the saying goes, "Art is a reflection of society," and as an art, choral music reflects societal values and trends. First of all, the Internet now provides choral conductors with unprecedented access to repertoire lists, historical practice, information on conducting and teaching, and other relevant research more than ever before.

A second trend is the implementation of repertoire standards. Many states are taking bold strides in updating and raising repertoire standards. "You can't make a purse out of a sow's ear" any easier than a conductor can elevate the level of a music program with substandard music or learning experiences. Students are best motivated to learn when the medium is worth learning.

The rise of community youth orchestras and choirs in the last two decades is an extremely positive trend of marked influence on all aspects of music making. It is like a sleeping giant that awakened. As members of these youth ensembles become adults, they often participate in community choruses, orchestras, college choirs, church and synagogue choirs, arts boards, and civic groups of various and sundry kinds. Children who participate in school and community music programs are, naturally, more likely to support and value the arts as adults, thus ensuring the future health and welfare of fine and performing arts throughout the country.

The deluge of multicultural music into the choral mainstream is another positive trend, even withstanding many contributions by non-authoritative sources. Of course, the choral art in this country has always enjoyed multiculturalism in the purest sense, that is, the music of Germany, Italy, Spain, England, France, and many more "cultures." But the recent infusion of music from New Zealand, Africa, China, and "lesser-represented cultures" has added a refreshing and not so familiar taste to the "repertoire pot," and it has had a dramatic revitalizing effect.

Lastly, parents today have less time to supervise after-school piano or instrument practice, transport children to lessons, attend concerts, and volunteer for school and community arts groups. This is a troubling phenomenon. However, I trust that the youth community arts movement, increased school repertoire standards, and the ever-increasing skill and competence of our many wonderful teachers in school music classrooms will serve as counterweights to this trend. People tend to find time for the things they value.

I feel the future of choral music is bright and will continue to flourish, thanks to the concerted efforts of those continuing its legacy. No business or discipline on the planet has a problem-free future. Our plight as composers, conductors, and administrators is to find solutions to those challenges, emphasize the positive, and find ways to strengthen our link in the human chain. We have just as much responsibility as Palestrina had in his time, as Bach had in his, as Brahms in his; now *we* are "up to the plate," and it is *our* time. Music history happens every passing minute. Future generations will look back at this time-link and ask, "What did *they* do to strengthen the chain?" Let us now build a legacy that will frame our time for history to view—to have a taste for high quality repertoire, a passion for dynamic leadership, and the rugged inner fortitude not to waver until the job is done. So be it.

J. Comprehensive List of Works for Choir
Larger Works:

American Rhapsody/American Christmas,
     SATB/brass/organ/timpani/percussion (or strings/timpani/
     percussion), (14:00), Alliance Music Publications
American Te Deum, SSA/piano/violin/cello/percussion, (20:00),
     Alliance Music Publications
Cantus Natalis, SATB/treble choir/brass (four trumpets, three
     trombones, tuba), percussion (two) and organ, (19:00), Alliance
     Music Publications

Flores del Agua (*Water Lilies*), (11:00), SATB/virtuoso piano, unpublished

Hodie! (*This Day*), SATB/brass/organ/timpani/percussion, (13:00), Mark Foster

Illuminaciones, mixed choir/treble choir/orchestra, (40:00), unpublished

Mixed Chorus:

A Red, Red Rose, SATB/piano, Alliance Music Publications

A Sun Day Hymn, SATB/organ, Mark Foster

All My Heart This Night Rejoices, SATB/unaccompanied, Colla Voce Music

All So Still, SATB/unaccompanied, Mark Foster

Amor de Mi Alma, SATB/unaccompanied, Walton

Arise, My Love, My Fair One, SATB/piano, Colla Voce Music

Cantate Domino, SATB/tambourine, Mark Foster

Caritas et Amor, SSATBB/unaccompanied, Alliance Music Publications

Come Dwell in Solomon's Walls, SATB/piano (orchestral accompanied available), MorningStar Music Publishing

Come into My Garden, SATB/piano, Colla Voce Music

Come to Me, My Love, SATB/oboe, Colla Voce Music

Come, Let Us Sing a Song for Joy, SATB/piano (optional brass), Mark Foster

Dona Nobis Pacem, SATB/organ (piano), Mark Foster

Everywhere Christmas Tonight, SATB/unaccompanied, Mark Foster

Gaelic Blessing (Tonn Leat), SATB/organ, unpublished

Goin' to the Auction, SATB/unaccompanied, Mark Foster

Homeland, SATB/piano (brass quintet/percussion available or full orchestra), Colla Voce Music

How Can I Keep From Singing?, SSATBB/unaccompanied, Alliance Music Publications

I Am Not Yours, SATBB/unaccompanied, Walton

In Time of Silver Rain, SATB/piano four hands/percussion, Colla Voce Music

Inscription of Hope, SATB/piano (oboe/strings available), Heritage Music Press

Joy Shall Be Yours in the Morning, SATB/unaccompanied, Mark Foster

Lamb of God, Grant Us Peace, SATB/organ (piano), Mark Foster

Lamentaciones de Jeremias, SATB/piano, Alliance Music Publications

Let Us Go into the House of the Lord, SATB/organ, Mark Foster

Ode to Joy, SATB/piano four hands (optional percussion available for three or four players), Alliance Music Publications

Old Horatius Had a Farm, SATB/unaccompanied, Mark Foster

Omnia Sol, SATB/piano, Heritage Music Press

Prelude to Peace, SATB/piano, Colla Voce Music

Resonet in Laudibus, SATB/piano/snare, Mark Foster

Shall I Compare Thee to a Summer's Day?, SATB/piano, Alliance Music Publications

Sicut Cervus, double mixed choir/unaccompanied, Mark Foster

Song for the Earth, SATB/piano/flute, Colla Voce Music

Sure on This Shining Night, SATB/piano, Mark Foster

The Best of Rooms, SATB/organ, MorningStar Music Publishing

The Call, SATB/organ (piano), MorningStar Music Publishing

The Cloths of Heaven, SATB/piano, Colla Voce Music

The Conversion of Saul, SSAATTBB/unaccompanied, Alliance Music Publications

The Pasture, SATB/piano (orchestral version available), Colla Voce Music

There Is Sweet Music Here, SATBB/unaccompanied, Alliance Music Publications

Tournez, Tournez, SATB/piano/tambourine/bongos/cabassa/claves/temple blocks/vibraslap, Alliance Music Publications

We Beheld Once Again the Stars, double mixed choir/unaccompanied, Alliance Music Publications

Winter, SSATB/piano, Alliance Music Publications

Women's Chorus:

Dies Irae, SSA, piano, Alliance Music Publications

Homeland, SSA/piano (two instrumental versions available: brass and percussion and full orchestra), Colla Voce Music

I Had a Paint Box, SA/piano, Colla Voce Music

Inscription of Hope, SA/piano, Heritage Music Press

Laudamus Te, SSA/piano, Walton

Lux Aeterna, SA/organ (piano), Alliance Music Publications

Magnificat, SSAA/piano four hands, Alliance Music Publications

Omnia Sol, SSA/piano, Heritage Music Press

Psalm 23, SSA/piano/flute/oboe, Alliance Music Publications

Resonet in Laudibus, SA–SA/piano/snare, Mark Foster

Sanctus, SSA/organ, unpublished

The Poet Sings, SSA/piano, Heritage Music Press

There Is No Rose, SSA/piano/oboe, Alliance Music Publications

Men's Chorus:

Amor de Mi Alma, TTBB (optional piano), Walton

Dies Irae, TTBB/piano, Alliance Music Publications

Homeland, TTBB/ piano (optional brass/percussion/organ or full orchestra), Colla Voce Music

andré
Thomas

A. Biography

A ndré J. Thomas, the Owen F. Sellers Professor of Music, is director of choral activities and professor of choral music education at Florida State University. A previous faculty member at the University of Texas, Austin, Thomas holds degrees from Friends University (bachelor of arts), Northwestern University (master of music), and the University of Illinois (doctor of musical arts). He is in demand as a choral adjudicator, clinician, and director of honor/all-state choirs throughout the United States, Europe, Asia, New Zealand, and Australia.

Thomas has conducted choirs at the state, division, and national conventions of the Music Educators National Conference (MENC) and American Choral Directors Association (ACDA). His international conducting credits are extensive and include conductor/clinician for the International Federation of Choral Musicians, summer residency of the World Youth Choir in the Republic of China and the Philippines, winter residency of the World Youth Choir in Europe, and a premiere performance by an American choir (Florida State University Singers) in Vietnam. He has been the guest conductor of such distinguished ensembles as the Birmingham Symphony Orchestra in England and the Berlin Radio Choir in Germany.

Thomas has also distinguished himself as a composer/ arranger. Hinshaw Music Company, Mark Foster Music Company, Fitzsimmon Music Company, Lawson Gould, earth-songs, and Heritage Music Company all publish his compositions and arrangements. Thomas has produced two instructional videos, one on choral conducting with Rodney Eichenberger (*What They See Is What You Get*) and one on adolescent voices with Anton Armstrong (*Body, Mind, Spirit, Voice*). He is a past president of the Florida ACDA and also of the Southern Division of ACDA.

***

I think I probably chose a career in choral music when I was four years old, although I didn't realize it at the time. I went to the Tabernacle Baptist Church in Wichita, Kansas, with my mother, and then I would come home and "play church." I never played the part of the minister, but I banged on my toy piano and accompanied an imaginary choir. Somehow I knew then that "that was it"—it was what I was going to become.

I veered a little from my path toward becoming a choir director because my piano skills opened some other doors. While pursuing a master's degree in piano performance at Northwestern University, I was offered a contract to play with a professional orchestra. Only when I had to make a decision about what I really wanted to do with my life did it become quite clear to me that choral music was my true calling.

That decision led me back to Wichita to teach in the public schools; for me the world of choral music was found in teaching. It seemed obvious to everyone that being a teacher was what I would do with my life, and at the time it was all I needed because I enjoyed working with people and realizing how choral music made them feel.

The fact that I could get paid to teach choral music was somehow amazing to me. I took over the choirs at Tabernacle Baptist when I was fourteen years old and held that position until I left Wichita at age twenty-four. My first experience composing for choirs was for the musical pageant associated with the church's annual "homecoming" celebration. I had to create the production and composed some rather informal song transitions and new melodies for the choir. The fact that I had sort of dreamed up this music seemed a bit mystical to me. The choir also performed at the Century II Convention Center in Wichita in a production called *Dark Symphony* that was turned into a PBS pilot, so I wrote and arranged pieces for that program as well.

By the time I got to Friends University, I had very functional keyboard skills, which proved quite practical in the theory classes, where I learned about voice leading and basic composing skills. I took a choral arranging class taught by Elaine Meadows that really intrigued me. She introduced me to the Hawley Ades book *Choral Arranging*, which sort of lit a fire within me, but I didn't think seriously about arranging music again for a long time.

Composing became an absolute necessity for me during my first year of teaching junior high school when I first walked into that classroom and realized I didn't have any music that really fit the voices in front of me. I had to find something that they could sing. How was I going to motivate this really diverse group of kids? Immediately, my ear went to work, and my pencil started going. Of all of the pieces I wrote, I only sent one off for publication, and it was rejected. After that experience, I gave up on the idea of publishing any music. However, in 2005 I revisited the same tune ("Barbara Allen") and made a new arrangement, which is now in print

It wasn't until I met Don Hinshaw when I was teaching at the University of Texas that I revisited the idea of composing. I took a group of students from my methods class to a reading session, and when it was over Don thanked me for bringing my students to the session. My response was: "They need to find opportunities for new repertoire because they will be doing this the rest of their lives." Don gave me a funny look and said, "This is a strange question, but have you written any music?" I told him that I did have a piece. The year was 1982, and the piece was "Keep Your Lamps."

Around the same time, Colleen Kirk, the president of ACDA, asked me to do a session for the ACDA on beginning repertoire at a national convention. That convention was also the first meeting between MENC and TMEA since they had split. Don asked me when the session was, and I told him it was in about a month. He said, "Send me that 'Lamps' piece tomorrow, and I will have it ready for your ACDA session." Don had never seen the piece, and he had just agreed to publish it in less than a week. That piece has served us both quite well; "Keep Your Lamps" has never sold fewer than 15,000 copies a year. The amazing thing is that just when I think everybody in the world must know this piece it will have a year like 2005 and sell 35,000 copies. I guess it means that a new group of people or a new generation of choral directors has rediscovered the piece.

B. The Creative Process

Here is a "strange" example of how things seem to come to me. I like a writer by the name of Wayne Dyer, and I was listening to one of his books on tape. My ears perked up when he quoted William Blake, and I knew that poem would be the text of my next composition. I don't know when it will be written, but the text is already chosen.

Sometimes a tune will snap into my head. For instance, I have a piece called "Rockin' Jerusalem" that was literally written between airport terminals A and C. I didn't have manuscript paper to write it on and was sure I would forget it, so I pulled out my checkbook and scratched down the pitches for the first eight-measure phrase in the register. I had no idea what to do with this "hook" that was in my head, but I knew it was a keeper. In the meantime, the FSU University Singers had been invited to sing at the National Cathedral. They wanted a program of entirely American music. As I started thinking of a text for that concert, I toyed with words like "Rumblin'" and "Rockin'," which were, for some reason, a perfect fit with the airport song I had written in the checkbook.

Lately, the inspiration for most of my new pieces has occurred while being stuck at home during a hurricane and its aftermath. My frightened dog stays on my lap, and since there is nothing else to do, we sit together and put down a few songs.

I am terribly fascinated with poet Langston Hughes. Because I like his works so much, I plan to write one more piece based on his poetry to complete a suite. He is indeed a great man, and those works need to be shared.

I can't really say I have a typical way of approaching a new piece of music. Some composers seem to evolve melodically, while others grow first harmonically. With me, it depends on the day. Sometimes I might hear a driving rhythm. Other days I seem to gravitate to a particular series of chords. I remember walking across the campus of Florida State with Earlene Rentz one day and humming the tune of "London Bridge Is Falling Down," singing it asymmetrically. She used my humming rendition of the song as the impetus for her arrangement of "London Bridge."

For me, composing is pretty organic, a process; once the words and music are in my head, I can immediately sit down and play the song. Sometimes I have to just sit quietly and stare at the text, while other times I will open up the computer and jot down ideas, like when I had just visited the Berlin Wall. Niel Lorenz had sent me a text called "Fences," and I knew the text had to have a propelling image. As I thought about structure, I wanted a forward-moving accompaniment and immediately thought of a toccata. Sitting at the computer, I pounded out a rhythm that was almost kinesthetic in the way it moved from my head to my fingers. The motion started the piece, and the text told me, "walls and spires"; images of the Berlin Wall flooded my head, and I envisioned many voices singing at once. When I asked myself who would be singing this piece, my first thought was the women's choir directed by Judy Bowers at FSU. I knew Judy had some very "healthy" voices in her choir, and I put that sound in my head. That was it. I wrote the entire piece without ever sitting down to a piano keyboard to play it.

"I Hear America Singing" was a strange animal; it was one of those commissioned pieces that I knew about but could not seem to get started. For some composers, their lives center around their compositions. My life does not. At the time I was commissioned to write "I Hear America Singing," I had two little children, I was running a choral program at FSU, and I was doing a lot of guest conducting. The commission just seemed to lurk over my head—like a huge monkey on my back. The piece was going to be performed by an ACDA honor choir, and it had to be done by January to pass out to the students. They didn't have any stipulation except that the piece would close the honor choir performance. I procrastinated almost a year until the Christmas holiday.

My wife, Portia, had finally gotten fed up with me and locked me in my office and said, "You are going to write this piece. I will send you food, but you are not coming out until it is finished." At that point, I had decided the text would be Walt Whitman's poem "I Hear America Singing." The published work that people know today is nothing like the first draft of that piece. With the first draft, somehow my ego had taken over. I knew the piece was going to be premiered at an ACDA national convention, so I had in my mind that the composition needed to somehow be significant. Every composer that I thought was significant was represented in the first draft. When I played it for Portia, she looked at me and said, "It stinks."

I looked back at her with the patience that only comes with years of marriage and said, "And . . . anything more besides it stinks?"

She said, "It's not you. It sounds like ten different people." And the truth is, that is exactly what it was. She said, "What about this text? How much of it really speaks to you?"

Well, the truth is that only certain parts of the text really spoke to me. I ended up only using the first line of the poem. Then I started thinking about the things that resonate with me. The list included love of kids, which always has been there, love of country, and love of my background and experiences.

Portia said, "Why don't you write about that?" So, it was back into the office, which is when the idea of "Walk Together

Children" came to me. I didn't want the traditional version, so I started with the closing line, "Great camp meeting in the promised land." That rhythm became the impetus for the whole piece.

I am a pretty lucky man. My first piece was published in 1982, and twenty-four years later nothing is permanently out of print. I am truly humbled by that success. It makes me realize that different pieces appeal to different people. I am not embarrassed by anything I've written; my pieces paint a picture of who I was at different times in my career. Some people like the early pieces better than my current compositions, and that is perfectly fine. I think I am heading in some different directions.

I no longer feel the need to write everybody's "closer." I want to feel free to write some pieces that are not up-tempo and that will showcase my quiet side. "I Dream a World," for example, has had some amazing sales. I was fortunate to have that piece performed by a choir of 700 men and boys at the World Symposium of Choral Music. Just recently, CNN news ran a tribute to Rosa Parks and "I Dream a World" was part of that broadcast, which to me seemed totally appropriate.

C. The Relationship Between Text and Music

Most of the time, the text is the starting point. Very rarely does the melody come to me before I have a text to go with it . . . unless it is scribbled in my checkbook.

It is not at all easy to come up with the right music. Some writers seem to have that gift; I just have to wait. There is no formula for how long it will take. Sometimes the music just happens, and sometimes I really have to hold off and let the text sit and simmer for a while. "Hold Fast to Dreams" stayed in the back of my mind for almost a year. I knew I loved the text, and as it developed and I decided on the group that was going to perform the piece, the music began to take shape. I am still not convinced that it is the definitive setting of that text, but I do feel it has something to say to the listener.

I attempt to write music that is singable for the great masses of people. I have not written anything that comes across as, "This is my artistic temperament. Good luck and see what you can do with this." I have a lot of people read my music before I send it to final press. I'll drag students into my office and say, "Sing this."

Obviously, a good portion of my work is the arrangement of spirituals, so I am always glancing through materials for source work. I keep the Nathaniel Dett anthology—three volumes of Negro spirituals—beside my desk, and I frequently glance through it for source ideas. I have several books of spiritual texts and some books of poetry by black authors. One of those books devotes the first two chapters to spirituals. While reading Eileen Southern's book as a reminder of style, I came across "Follow the Drinking Gourd." At the same time my daughter was reading a children's book about the "Drinking Gourd."

I can't ignore that kind of coincidence; it became the text for my next commissioned piece. The "Drinking Gourd" was written for the combined men's, women's, and mixed choirs to close an Indiana convention. As I recall, there was a huge snowstorm the night of the performance, and half the kids made it there, so the piece wasn't quite as glorious as I originally pictured it in my head, but it still was extremely fulfilling to hear those young people sing it.

D. Views from the Composer to the Conductor Pertaining to Score Study and Preparation

There are several issues here. Perhaps I am sensitive to this topic because I am a conductor and I continuously work with conductors in festivals around the world. Sometimes conductors can be quite forward or aggressive in their interpretations, or they feel quite free to make decisions that may not be consistent with the composer's original intent. Some conductors even go so far as to recompose a piece. I have never felt compelled to do that with another composer's work. If I don't particularly like a piece, I will program something else. I feel like I owe it to the composer to try to understand the music, the style, and what the composer is trying to say.

I don't have a definite style because I don't want every piece to sound the same. Even within the spiritual genre, "Keep Your Lamps" has a very distinct sound compared to "When the Trumpets Sound," and those should both have a different feel than "Band of Angels." Sometimes I can hear a jazz influence in my works; some have a gospel style, and others hearken back to the traditional form of the spiritual.

William Dawson and I once had a discussion on the appropriate compositional practices for spirituals. He said to me after "Keep Your Lamps" came out, "You know, the music is alright, but it just doesn't have enough counterpoint." I personally didn't think the slaves were out in the field singing in fugues, but in deference to Mr. Dawson, I added some counterpoint to the last few pages of "Rockin' Jerusalem."

The conductor should look carefully at the composer's markings and instructions in the music. If the composer has included jazz elements, then the conductor has some freedom to interpret the music in a certain way. Sometimes, tempo can also be

216

subjective. Anton Armstrong has conducted "Keep Your Lamps" numerous times. Each time Anton conducts this song, he interprets it a little differently. His initial performance tempo was slower han I had imagined; however, it was effective. In subsequent performances his tempo has been faster. It is amazing how a composer can hear a different tempo and still feel the piece is effective or improved. Sergei Rachmaninoff once did the same thing; after he heard his second piano concerto in the concert hall, the new acoustic caused him to change the tempo.

I ask the conductor to try to understand the composer's intent and transmit that intent with what you have available. I used to think conductors were misinterpreting every piece of mine, but that was helpful in a way because as a young composer it helped me to understand how people interpret things differently. I would write an "agitated' marking in a piano part, and then I would hear Jerry Lee Lewis on the keyboard at various performances! Composers can only put symbols on paper to represent the sound in their head, but I have come to realize those symbols often don't mean the same thing to me as they do to somebody else. I keep working to make sure my intent is clear.

E. The Relationship Between the Composer and the Commissioning Party

I have composed almost all of my pieces when a friend, a family member, or I have needed a special piece to perform. There have been a few commissions along the way, but it is not something I do very often. Commissions are a totally different animal, and I will only accept commissions under extenuating circumstances.

I have not done any commissions in the last year. The last commission that I accepted was for the Kansas Choral Directors

Association almost two years ago, as a tribute to my mentor, Harold Decker. It now seems almost ironic that the source material was "Barbara Allen," the tune of the first piece I submitted and couldn't get published.

Although I still get asked to write commissions, I don't often take them. But I am still actively conducting; most places invite me to include my "latest piece" on the program. This gives me a built-in audience for a piece and virtually guarantees the publisher that multiple copies of the composition will be purchased.

The problem with commissions, for me, is that a group of people are dependent on me to meet a deadline. I have more than enough deadlines in my life. To add another deadline and not be able to meet it would be catastrophic for me. I would hate to give my word and not be able to live up to that verbal or written handshake. I can't say that I won't ever take another commission, because I may, but I will think about it very carefully because I can't always meet the imposed deadline.

The other thing about commissions is that I sometimes feel confined by certain expectations. One piece I wrote was commissioned to include references to nature, the black experience, and the Native American way of life and also a hymn and something from the New Testament. This piece, "The Kingdom," has a "Fruits of the Spirit" from the New Testament, a psalm setting, and Chief Seattle's text—that all things in nature are connected—included in it; that is how that piece came together.

Whether a piece is commissioned or not, I don't write anything I don't think will be performed. Sometimes I write for an imaginary choir, which is why I make a point of having somebody read through my pieces early in the process, such as the student chapter of ACDA or one of the choirs at FSU. I have probably conducted everything I have written somewhere along the line.

F. Views on the Teaching of Composition and How to Mentor the Young Composer

I recently conducted a performance of choral music by FSU composers with the FSU Chamber Choir, and it was quite successful. Over the last ten years or so, students have brought their music in to have me take a look at it. I have had a number of students in the choral program who also compose, and my work has led to a lot of one-on-one mentoring of those students. I try to help them find their own language and figure out what works and what is readable.

Sometimes the advice is as simple as, "You cannot leave the sopranos on a high B-flat for that many measures, and did you realize all of those F-sharps are going to hit right on the break for some of those voice types?" They need reminders of some of the idiomatic aspects of choral writing. I try to get them to answer questions like, "How much time is needed to articulate a line like the one you have written?" If they are writing a piece with organ accompaniment, do they really want the voices at the same dynamic and pitch level as the organ? If not, then maybe they should open up the chords and get more spacing for the singers and listeners.

I meet with some students twice a week, while others only want to meet once a month or when they have something to show me. The whole idea is to lend them another set of ears and to guide them without influencing them too much. It is hard to help students fix something in their compositions without turning it into an André Thomas piece. I feel this work is important, but I am glad I don't do it all day because it is so difficult to balance the needs of the student with what I hear in the piece.

If a young composer truly wants to be successful, he or she needs to find a trustworthy person to provide the feedback necessary for him or her to grow. In the earlier part of the twentieth century, people would get on the plane and fly to France to study with Nadia Boulanger. Students truly need someone to analyze their writing and their style. There are composition teachers in every school, but students need to find somebody who is open and willing to let them grow in the direction they choose. Composers also need to know that it is okay to write a tune! Copland never apologized for writing a singable melody.

Young people often feel inclined to emulate certain composers. They may say, "I want to write like John Rutter" or "I want to find the set of chords that work for Morten Lauridsen," but what they really need to be asking is whether that really fits their compositional style. Young composers must, in the end, be true to themselves.

I also want to encourage choral publishers to take a chance on aspiring composers. The truth is, the first time I sent in a piece, I didn't get any response from the publishing company. I hope future young composers don't become discouraged by publishing companies that don't respond or reject submissions because sometimes this process can take a little time.

G. Individuals Who Were Especially Influential in My Development and Career

I would have to say all of my teachers were influential. In undergraduate school it was Elaine Meadows who provided the formal guidelines to my composition and arranging in a choral arranging class. She also introduced me to the Haley Ades arranging text that I still use as a reference.

I usually write because of an immediate need. For example, if Anton Armstrong needed a piece for something, well, I would write it. He has programmed a number of my pieces, including "Here's a Pretty Little Baby" and "I Hear America Singing" and those used in the St. Olaf Christmas festival—"Keep Your Lamps," "Go Where I Send Thee," and "Rise up Shepherds and Follow," which has certainly helped with their popularity and exposure.

Other conductors, like Rod Eichenberger, have frequently programmed my music with all-state choirs. The ACDA honor choir commission, all-state commissions, and some church group commissions have been very important in my career.

H. Twelve Works All Choral Conductors at All Levels Should Study

This is a very difficult question. Because of the vastness of our repertoire, it would be impossible to know all that is available, but I will just name a few works I consider to be important.

1. Giovanni Pierluigi da Palestrina: *Missa papae macelli*
2. Giovanni Gabrieli: "In excelsis"
3. J. S. Bach: *St. Matthew Passion*, *St. John Passion*, B Minor Mass, "Singet dem Herren"
4. George Frideric Handel: *Messiah*
5. W. A. Mozart: Requiem
6. Franz Joseph Haydn: *Creation*
7. Johannes Brahms: Requiem
8. Igor Stravinsky: *Symphony of Psalms*

9. Francis Poulenc: *Gloria*
10. Arthur Honneger: *King David*
11. Gabriel Fauré: Requiem
12. Ludwig van Beethoven: Ninth Symphony, *Missa solemnis*

I. The Future of Choral Music

I think that the exposure to folk and classical music from other countries has been the biggest positive change for the future of choral music. I also think the International Federation of Choral Musicians has been a considerable influence on American choral music.

To young writers, my best advice is: Keep writing. You never know what your legacy will be. Write if you have something to say!

J. Comprehensive List of Works for Choir
Mixed Voices:

African Noel, SATB, *a cappella*, Alfred Publishing Company

Band of Angels, SATB, piano, Lorenz Publishing Company

Beautiful City, SATB, piano, Lorenz Publishing Company

Death Is Gonna Lay His Cold Icy Hands on Me, SATB, piano, Shawnee Press

Deep River, SATB, *a cappella*, Lorenz Publishing Company

Fences, SATB, piano, Lorenz Publishing Company

Go Down 'n the Valley and Pray, SATB, *a cappella*, Lorenz Publishing Company

Go Where I Send Thee, SATB, piano, Shawnee Press

Goin' Up to Glory, SATB, piano, Lorenz Publishing Company

Great Day, SATB, piano, Fitzimmons Publishing Company

Heaven, SATB, piano, Shawnee Press

Here's a Pretty Little Baby, SATB with soprano/tenor solo, synthesizer, flute, percussion, bass, earthsongs

Hold Fast to Dreams, SATB, piano, Hinshaw Music

I Dream a World, SAB, three-part mixed choir, piano, Lorenz
    Publishing Company; SATB, piano, Lorenz Publishing Company

I Hear America Singing, SATB, also available as three-part mixed
    choir, piano with optional full orchestra (concert band),
    Lorenz Publishing Company

I Open My Mouth (I Won't Turn Back), SATB, piano, Hinshaw Music

I Will Sing Praises, SATB, Lorenz Publishing Company

I'm A-Rollin', SATB, piano, Hinshaw Music

I'm Gonna Sing, SATB, piano, Lorenz Publishing Company

If You're Happy/Amen, SATB, piano with optional
    performance/accompaniment CD, Lorenz Publishing Company

John Saw duh Numbuh, SATB, piano, Lorenz Publishing Company

Keep Your Lamps!, SATB, conga drums, Hinshaw Music

Kingdom (with Helena Barrington), SATB, piano, Hinshaw Music

Let Everything, SATB, Lorenz Publishing Company

Peter, Go Ring Dem Bells, SATB, Lorenz Publishing Company

Ride the Chariot, SATB, Hinshaw Music

Rise up, Shepherd and Follow, SATB, *a cappella*, Lorenz Publishing
    Company

Rockin' Jerusalem, SATB, piano, Shawnee Press

Swing Down Chariot, SATB, *a cappella*, Lorenz Publishing Company

The Drinking Gourd, SATB, piano, Lorenz Publishing Company

Walk in the Light, SATB (also available for unison/two-part choir),
    piano, Lorenz Publishing Company

Walk the Streets of Gold quoting "I Got Shoes" and "Golden Slippers,"
    SATB, piano, Lorenz Publishing Company

When the Trumpet Sounds, SATB, piano, Shawnee Press

Women's Chorus:

Barbara Allen, SSA, flute and piano, Lorenz Publishing Company

Fences, SSA, piano, Lorenz Publishing Company

Good News!, SSA, Lorenz Publishing Company

I Hear America Singing, two-part choir, piano with optional full
   orchestra (concert band), Lorenz Publishing Company
If You're Happy/Amen, two-part treble and piano with optional
   performance/accompaniment CD, Lorenz Publishing Company
I'm Gonna Sing, SSA, piano, Lorenz Publishing Company
John Saw duh Numbuh, SSAA, piano, Lorenz Publishing Company
Keep Your Lamps, SSA, piano, Hinshaw Music
The Drinking Gourd, two-part with optional flute, Lorenz Publishing
   Company

Men's Chorus:

Barbara Allen, TTB/TBB, flute and piano, Lorenz Publishing Company
Goin' Up to Glory, TTBB, piano, Lorenz Publishing Company
Good News!, TTB/TBB, Lorenz Publishing Company
Heaven, TTBB, piano, Shawnee Press
Swing Down Chariot, TTBB, *a cappella*, Lorenz Publishing Company

chapter 10

gwyneth
Walker

A. Biography

G wyneth Walker (b. 1947) is a graduate of Brown University and the Hartt School of Music. She holds bachelor of art, master of music, and doctor of musical arts degrees in music composition. A former faculty member of the Oberlin College Conservatory, she resigned from academic employment in 1982 to pursue a career as a full-time composer. She now lives on a dairy farm in Braintree, Vermont.

Walker's catalogue includes more than one hundred and fifty commissioned works for orchestra, band, chorus, and chamber ensembles. Her works have been performed in venues that vary widely—from barns to Carnegie Hall—and by a wide range of musicians—from amateur singers to professional orchestras. Walker's entire career has been marked by her interest in writing music in a variety of genres.

Gwyneth Walker received the Year 2000 "Lifetime Achievement Award" from the Vermont Arts Council. She also received the Raymond Brock Memorial Commission from the American Choral Directors Association in 1998. Her Web site, www.gwynethwalker.com, provides detailed information about all of her compositions.

***

I feel that I inherited many attributes and qualities from my parents that are useful for being a composer. My father was a very inventive person—he never felt the need to be conventional—and my mother, although not a professional musician, had a good musical ear.

I come from a long line of Quakers. In the Quaker faith both men and women are equal—that is a good outlook to inherit as well. I have a practical and down-to-earth personality, and I try to treat everyone equally, which is a basic Quaker philosophy.

I started composing music when I was two years old. My older sister began taking piano lessons when she was in first grade. In the evenings, when she was practicing and I was supposed to be falling asleep upstairs, I remember hearing the sound of the piano being played directly under my room. It was so exciting that the next morning, when my sister was in school, I climbed up on the piano bench and started making my own sounds. I continued to do this every day! Over time, I became better at emulating what my sister had been playing, and I also started creating my own music at the piano.

By the time I was in first grade, I had my own orchestra of friends. Each Monday, they came to my house to perform my latest (brief) composition, using the array of instruments in my house. Composing music for others to play and sing has always been my favorite activity!

In high school, I played guitar and sang in a folk group for which I wrote all of the choral arrangements. Unlike some groups of this sort that learn the music by rote, we all read music quite well. Thus, I notated all of these arrangements. Later, when I was an undergraduate at Brown University, I was in a similar vocal group for which I also wrote arrangements. This was how I earned my spending money during my college years.

I started writing music at such a young age that I found my musical voice very early on. Outside influences do not easily affect me. I am grateful to Ron Nelson and Paul Nelson, my professors at Brown University, for the technical training they each gave me in school; however, I would not say that these teachers influenced my style. Similarly, my composition teacher at the Hartt School of Music, Arnold Franchetti, let me develop as an individual.

B. The Creative Process

A. The Process of Composing Music

People who choose to become creative writers, whether in words or music, do not lack inspiration and ideas, but many have trouble finding the time to write everything down. If one does not have imagination, I would not recommend becoming a composer!

I have learned over the years what sorts of works and genres best suit my style and showcase my skills. At this point in my career I have a long list of works I would like to write. When somebody contacts me to inquire about a commission, I check to see if their request matches something that is already on my list. If it does, then we are pursuing a work that is mutually beneficial.

The actual "beginning" of the piece is when the project is conceived and added to my schedule. It usually takes several years for me to start a new commission because I have other works on my schedule. The commissioning ensemble and I determine when the piece is needed, and then, during those two or so years of lead time before the composing begins, we can discuss the concept behind the work. As the deadline gets closer, I start jotting down musical ideas. When the time comes to write the piece, I am therefore not starting from scratch. In fact, I am usually quite eager to start putting notes to page, because the piece is all planned out and ready to go. I have already envisioned the shape, the concept, and the form of the piece.

Before I put pencil to paper, I have a good idea of the form, a broad concept for the tonalities of the piece, and basic motivic ideas. One of the best examples is my choral work "I Thank You God" (1998) for SSA chorus and piano for which I have written a musical analysis (posted on my Web site). I planned the overall tonal scheme carefully. The music starts from a low C and moves from a C minor modality through increasingly distant keys up to E-flat minor before opening into a radiant C major. This tonal voyage was constructed before I began the work.

Some pieces come more easily than others, and I think any writer would agree. Sometimes it depends on my mood or how rested I am. As I explained, I must have a plan before I begin writing on paper, and it may take a shorter or longer amount of time to decide upon a satisfactory plan. I evaluate different approaches and consider each for some time. I might go for a walk or get away from my house for a little while and then come back to test my different ideas. Once I have decided upon the concept, I start to commit notes to paper.

B. A Daily Routine

I have a fairly strict regimen for composing, as many composers do. As I read Benjamin Britten's biography, I was interested to learn that his schedule was very much like mine. I wake up in the morning—hopefully rested—and before I start writing, I will answer a few communications, because my mind is not totally energized for composing. By around 10 a.m. I am definitely ready to compose music. I turn the computer off and set to work for about four hours. Since I compose each day, I find that four hours is about the right amount of time for the energy I have to be creative.

Then I get up from the writing desk and do something else—play tennis, run errands, or anything that is a change of pace from the job of writing. When I come home, I return to the business of being an "administrator" for my compositions. I spend at least four hours a day on the communication aspect of my musical career. This involves exchanging letters with people for whom I am writing, with my publishers, with my webmaster, or answering the many inquires that arrive from individuals and groups who are performing my existing compositions. After that, I often spend some time editing or proofreading in the evenings.

I maintain this schedule seven days a week. My neighbors say that I "keep my hours"—just like in a monastery! And indeed I really do. I follow my daily routine religiously.

C. Craft and Methods

The process of arranging preexisting musical material interests me, although I do not specialize in this genre. Most of my works are newly composed, using original musical themes and ideas I have developed myself. However, I am intrigued by the idea of taking musical ideas from the past and looking at them in a contemporary way. The many approaches to creating arrangements range from rather straightforward transcriptions to idiosyncratic "departures" in the manner of Charles Ives. In my own work, I tend to lean toward the latter. This is not by choice so much as by personality; I find it impossible to simply recreate what has already been done, and I seem to find humor and character hiding behind almost any musical gesture!

It is thus my inclination and pleasure to seek out what I feel to be the essence and charm of each song and then try to enhance these traits through new adaptations. When I do an arrangement, the finished product is usually so different from the original that it becomes almost like a new piece. I "go to town" with it!

Take, for example, "Every Night (When the Sun Goes Down)" (1996) for SATB chorus, unaccompanied. I wrote the last two verses of that piece in memory of my father. I put much into the arrangement that was not in the original tune or lyrics at all, such as the new words I added to the ending of the song. So I prefer to call my arrangements contemporary adaptations. They are musical "excursions" or new presentations of the material. The adaptation brings something new to the song.

I enjoy writing for chorus and orchestra combined. However, the problem with this genre is that sometimes it is hard for the audience to understand the words because the chorus usually stands behind the orchestra. So I feel that if I start with lyrics that are somewhat familiar, such as those of a well-known song, the words will hopefully be better understood. Because of these logistical problems, I sometimes choose to create an arrangement rather than an original work in this genre. *The River Songs* and *New Millennium Suite* are examples of this approach.

Writing music is a craft, a skill that is carefully developed over years of training and practice. The composer is thus a craftsperson and should take pride in a "job well done" and "an honest day's work." Shortcuts to the compositional process are generally not effective! The composer and the performers intuitively know when a work is well written. The form is apparent, the message is discernible, and the writing is idiomatic enough to reflect knowledge of the instruments and voices involved. Originality combined with technical mastery produces a mature musical language.

Writing music is never easy, even for accomplished composers with professional careers. Time is needed for reflection, criticism, and experimentation, which allows the imagination to "play." A good composer is constantly challenging him- or herself to seek greater mastery of the craft. The voice of integrity lies in the pursuit of beauty.

C. The Relationship Between Text and Music

When I write choral or vocal music, the search for the text comes first. I do not usually write the words for my compositions. In my mind, I have the basic nature of the idea I am seeking. I first need to find the right poetry, then once I select the poems, I create the music.

When I set poetry to music, I focus on the central images in the poem. To me, poetry is not simply words, it is the images the words create. Thus, it is important that these poetic images translate clearly into musical expression. Often, the accompaniment is the central means of creating the imagery. The tenor of the poem may be established within the opening measures of accompaniment. The vocal lines also participate in some musical imagery, but their primary function is to convey the words.

The song must have a cogent and dramatic form of its own. The form of the song may mirror that of the poem, or it may transcend the poem. However, the music should always stand alone as a well-constructed entity, which is why I always establish the overall shape of the song before I start to compose.

As I form the concept of a new piece, the tonal plan seems to evolve naturally. The composer must know both what they want to say in a piece and how they want to say it. Sometimes the "how" is reflected in the tonalities, phrase shapes, and the return of melodies or rhythms. These are the various means to an end. I shape the musical presentation to try to convey the message of that poem. I do not take a poem, form some images in my mind, then start with the first word and go straight to the last. I try to let the words suggest the nature of the piece, and then I shape it myself. This is the composer's role.

I am a composer who values energy, beauty, humor, spirituality, and familiarity in music. I seek these qualities when I look for new texts. Take, for example, *Songs for Women's Voices* (1992) for SSA chorus and piano (or chamber orchestra). These six songs are based on poems by May Swenson (1919–89). Although all the poems speak with her poetic voice, each poem has a different message. One song uses a spiritual poem titled "The Name Is Changeless." "I Will Be Earth" is a love poem, and "Women Should Be Pedestals" is a humorous and feminist song. I like this variety.

I am always reading poetry and am constantly looking for poems I feel would make good musical settings. This way, when I am asked to write a new choral work, I already have something in mind. The search is not easy. Not all contemporary poetry speaks to me, but when I find writing that is beautiful, comprehensible, imaginative, perhaps humorous or spiritual, and subtle, I set this aside for a potential musical project.

Even though I know what I like in poetry, the poems I choose are not all "the same." A good example is the poetry of Lucille Clifton, which I have set in various works, including a cycle for unaccompanied women's chorus called *My Girls*. I first discovered Lucille Clifton's poetry fifteen years ago in a

Connecticut library and immediately loved the poems. She has a wonderful sense of humor and a very deep expression about her life. However, her style is very different from other poets'. You could find no greater contrast between "Sisters" and some of the May Swenson poems I have set. I like them all. I love American poetry anywhere I can find it. Many times the poems I use are somewhat obscure, but if I keep my eyes and ears open I encounter some fine American poets.

D. Views from the Composer to the Conductor Pertaining to Score Study and Preparation

Musicians who were not involved in the initial creative process (meaning they did not commission the pieces themselves) or who have never met me often perform my music. They may have picked up a piece at a reading session or heard it in a "new issue" packet, on a recording, or at a performance of another chorus.

One thing I have learned over the years is the importance of putting specific instructions on the page. This helps the conductor to render my musical intentions as accurately as possible. The metronome markings, articulations, dynamics, phrasing, program notes, and performance notes all help to create a performance that is as close as it can be to what I had in mind. It really is the composer's job to explain the nature of the work, whether in performance notes at the front of the score or through musical notation—some of both are often necessary.

All of my choral music is commissioned, and thus I am always writing each work for a specific chorus. Sometimes I know the group from past collaborations, but often I do not. If I do not know the group already, I will certainly ask the choral director for some information about the ensemble. I try to listen to

CDs they may have made and sometimes travel to hear them in concert. After I get an idea of the general nature of the group, I decide what kind of a work I can create that they will enjoy. At the same time, I try to write a piece that can be performed by other choruses after the music is premiered and published.

About performances: I believe that all composers can gain many performances of their music if the music is playable, communicative, and well written—and if the composer is organized enough to have the music available when requested. Meeting performers at concerts is also important. I feel that composers cannot live entirely in their own world. Music is a communicative and social language. Composers, performers, and audiences all need each other for the art to survive.

E. The Relationship Between the Composer and the Commissioning Party

As a Quaker-egalitarian artist, I have the perspective that all music has equal worth. The people who commission the music are of equal value to me; I do not give more time to a work for professional musicians than to a work for amateur musicians. Rather, I treat all of my commissions with the same professionalism and seriousness. I try to attend all the premieres of my compositions, whether they be with a school group or a professional ensemble; that is just my egalitarian approach.

I feel that every composer should be able to get their work performed if they collaborate with local ensembles. Most music making in the United States is done in churches, schools, and community concert halls, which is where we, as composers, should direct most of our energy. I like variety; when I am writing for different ensembles and choruses, I hope that my composing list includes the smaller, less skilled groups, right up through the top professional groups. I am happy to accept a variety of commissions and feel it is valuable to write for the local players.

In 1986, at a time when my musical career seemed to be progressing at a healthy pace, I felt that it was time to get everything on my shelves in order. Going back into the older music is a painful process, but one cannot move forward as long as the past is untended. I have talked to some other composers who have tried to do this, and we agree that it is frustrating to be dealing with the old and not creating the new. No fun at all!

I divided my catalog into three categories. The first category included the works that were in good shape—either ready to be engraved or already engraved. The second category comprised the works that I felt need never reach the public's eye—such as early student works, personal works, or gifts.

The third category was the most time-consuming. These were works from the past that, with some effort, could be improved enough to warrant inclusion in my catalog. I laid out all of the scores and, over the next ten months, revised each of them to the point of being ready for engraving. I am very glad I did this, because some of these works are strong pieces in my catalog.

I have a support system of professionals that makes my career possible. The music copyist who enters all of my music into the Finale format and I definitely work hand in hand. I know how to use Finale but prefer to write out the music by hand. That way, I can write anything I want and not worry about how the computer will deal with it. If I want to write an extended section without barlines, for example, I do not have to worry about computer copying complexities. Writing by hand frees my mind to create the best possible music.

And then there are the two publishers: E. C. Schirmer (for choral and vocal music) and MMB Music (for chamber and orchestral music). I also work with a webmaster to maintain my Web site. This is definitely a group enterprise.

I think that it helps to have a fairly good business sense if you want to make a living as a composer. Not everybody has that nature, but if you want to be a one-woman business (an entrepreneur), you have to be fairly practical and organized.

F. Views on the Teaching of Composition and How to Mentor the Young Composer

The model curriculum would begin with a very good background in music fundamentals. Students must know how to notate music, and by that I mean selecting the right meter for the rhythm, understanding key relationships for writing tonal music, and developing a vocabulary for making choices when writing non-tonal music. Basic musicianship goes a long way.

After a solid grounding in fundamentals, I would suggest that student and teacher examine diverse repertoire together. Perhaps they might discuss what they feel makes a certain work successful or any apparent flaws within the piece.

I don't think creativity can be taught. And "over-teaching" can be dangerous. I know of a composition teacher whose students ended up writing music that sounded like his. The teacher had a very strong personality, and these students were in their formative years and susceptible to his influence. The teacher's imposing personality overwhelmed the students, and they never found their voice. It is indeed hard to teach composition!

My advice to young people who are seeking a career in composition includes two basic points:

1. Pray that this is the right career for you—because you cannot wander into this without a lot of backing and support from the inside out. Ask yourself if this is really what you feel is right for you, both professionally and personally. What sort of a support system do you have? I would not have been able to sustain my career without a strong faith and friends and colleagues who believe in me.

2. Learn to compose for different mediums. A composer who writes for chorus should also learn to write for instruments. You may be writing for chorus and orchestra someday, so you should study orchestral writing while you are in school, or you will be continually haunted by this lack of training.

The life of a composer can be exciting as well as discouraging, beautiful as well as disappointing, exhilarating as well as exhausting. A few important words come to mind for young composers: patience, persistence, experimentation, struggle, self-motivation, faith, and courage.

Composers need patience to complete a work, especially a large-scale work. You cannot write everything in one sitting. Patience is valuable in career development. Remember that composers and performers often program repertoire years in advance. They may like your music but do not yet have the opportunity to program it. Be patient.

Be persistent! Keep composing and trying to get your music into the hands of performers. Learn about the world of music. This is a lifelong commitment. Believe in yourself. Write with your own voice, using your experiences and your values. Put all of yourself—your energy, love of life, and sense of humor—in your music and make it sound like "you."

Experiment with different genres, and try writing for various ensembles. Be open-minded while deciding which path is right for you. Youth is the time for experimentation.

Face your inner struggles, whatever they may be. Struggle with your self-doubt, lack of family support, or lack of a strong mentor. Struggle with your isolation and to get your music heard. Self-motivation is a powerful force (a writer must write!). There is a well-known "fear of the blank page." Self-doubt is magnified during long hours in solitude. Continue to struggle with yourself during the process of creating music.

Faith is an individual matter, but it must be part of your reason for writing. Spiritual energy is vital to creativity.

Perhaps courage should be considered the foremost trait needed by a composer: The courage to create and to put your music out for public listening. Courage to speak your true thoughts and feelings. Composers also need the courage to withstand being misunderstood by the community at large. Although there may be difficult moments, the gratification of creating something of beauty, which is shared and valued, outweighs the negative aspects. The one great joy that surpasses all others is the joy of forming a single musical thought and putting it down on paper. That is why you must compose music!

G. Individuals Who Were Especially Influential in My Development and Career

Not many people have influenced my career. I taught myself how to write music, and I have basically formed my own musical language. I am not somebody who is easily influenced by others—if I were, I would have given up composing years ago. People have told me that women should not write music. I could have listened to them, but I am still writing. My Quaker faith has helped me to persevere.

My colleagues have been the most helpful in my career. During my high school and college years, I sang in vocal octets for which I wrote the arrangements. My friends believed in my abilities, and we rehearsed together every day. During my last two years of high school and all throughout college, I was surrounded by my singing group friends. Their support gave me confidence as a composer, and their daily performance of my music helped me develop my skills.

Teachers gave me encouragement, but I do not believe they heavily influenced me. At the Hartt School of Music, my teacher Arnold Franchetti definitely believed in me and strongly supported my writing.

In some ways, audiences have influenced my compositions. The music I write exists very much inside my imagination; yet when the music is performed for an audience and it becomes evident that the music has reached the audience, this emboldens me to continue to put more of my feelings and imagination into my writing because I know that someone is listening. As I become more aware of how to communicate with the listener, I am better able to shape my musical messages. I care that people are listening, and I definitely keep them in mind when composing.

H. Ten Works All Choral Conductors at All Levels Should Study

I have decided to pass on this question. I am not a choral expert, and I am not that highly trained. I will let the other people in the book answer this question.

I. The Future of Choral Music

Human beings will always want to sing, so choral music definitely has a future. People like to get together and sing in a chorus and want music that is readily singable. I do not think the repertoire is going to get "more and more advanced" and replace tonal music. Nor will machines make all of the music!

I want to caution young composers about writing computer music instead of live music. The immediate sounds that MIDI or the computer can generate may be fascinating, but young, talented composers need to continue writing music for live performers. People will always want to sing and play, and it is important to maintain the flow of new ideas and new musical styles from the minds of composers into the hands of performers.

J. Comprehensive List of Works for Choir
Mixed Chorus Unaccompanied:

Chords of Love (2002, 3:45) ECS#6238, SATB, treble voices,
    traditional text (adapted by the composer)

Christ-Child's Lullaby (1988, 4:30) ECS#4380, SATB, alto solo,
    traditional text

Directions for Singing (2003, 7:00) GW, SATB, text by John Wesley
    (adapted by the composer)

Every Night (When the Sun Goes Down) (1996, 4:00) ECS#5135,
    SATB, traditional text

For Ever and Ever (1986, 3:00) ECS#4316, SATB, soprano solo, text
    from the Bible (The Lord's Prayer)

Give Over Thine Own Willing (1997, 3:45) ECS#5252, SATB, text
    adapted from the writings of Isaac Pennington by Paul Lacey

God's Grandeur (2002, 7:00) ECS#6046, SATB, texts by Gerald
    Manley Hopkins

If Ever Two Were One (2003, 3:15) ECS#6227, SATB, text by Anne
   Bradstreet (adapted by the composer)
Motherless Child (1996, 5:00) ECS#5131, SATB, traditional text
Peace Like a River (1989, 2:30) ECS#4485, SATB, traditional text
Sounding Joy (1985, 2:00) ECS#4318, SATB, text from the Bible
   (Psalm 95)
The Right to Vote (1998, 4:15) GW, SATB, text by Gwyneth Walker
The Road Goes Ever On (2006, 2:30) GW, SATB, text by J. R. R.
   Tolkien
The Troubled Sweet of Her (1978, 2:45) ECS#4307, SATB, optional
   solo SATB, male speaker) text by Amante
This Train (1997, 3:45) ECS#5189, SATB, traditional text (adapted
   by the composer)
Two Prayers from *The Golden Harp* (1999, 4:00) MMB#X940020,
   SATB, text by Rabindranath Tagore

Mixed Chorus with Piano Accompaniment:

A Heart in Hiding (2006, 16:00) GW, SATB, mezzo-soprano solo,
   piano, texts by Emily Dickinson
An Hour to Dance: No. 1 – Key Ring (1998, 2:30) ECS#5282, SATB,
   piano
An Hour to Dance: No. 2 – Summary by the Pawns (1998, 2:40)
   ECS#5283, SATB, piano
An Hour to Dance: No. 3 – The April Lovers (1998, 3:00) ECS#5284,
   SATB, piano
An Hour to Dance: No. 4 – An Hour to Dance (1998, 3:30)
   ECS#5285, SATB, piano
An Hour to Dance: No. 5 – Slow Scythe (1998, 3:00) ECS#5286,
   SATB, piano
An Hour to Dance: No. 6 – White Darkness (1998, 2:00) ECS#5287,
   SATB, piano
An Hour to Dance: No. 7 – Take My Hand (1998, 4:15) ECS#5288,
   SATB, soprano solo, piano, texts by Virginia Hamilton Adair

As a Branch in May (1983, 3:30) ECS#4888, SATB, piano, text by
  Gwyneth Walker

Cheek to Cheek (1978, 1:00) ECS#4308, SATB, piano, text by Carll
  Tucker

Every Life Shall Be a Song (2005, 3:00) GW, SATB, piano, John
  Addington Symonds (adapted by the composer)

Harlem Songs: No. 1 – Spirituals (2000, 3:45) ECS#5769, SATB, piano

Harlem Songs: No. 2 – Harlem Night Song (2000, 3:15) ECS#5770,
  SATB, piano

Harlem Songs: No. 3 – Tambourines (2000, 3:45) ECS#5771, SATB,
  piano, texts by Langston Hughes

How Can I Keep from Singing? (1995, 3:30) ECS#5100, SATB, piano,
  traditional text, Quaker hymn

I Thank You God (2002, 4:00) ECS#5977, SATB, piano, text by E. E.
  Cummings

I Will Be Earth (1992, 2:30) ECS#4887, SSATB, piano, text by May
  Swenson

Let Music Fill the Air (2003, 4:00) ECS#6363, SATB, piano
  (text adapted by composers from multiple sources)

Long Ago Lady (1984, 4:30) GW, SATB, piano, text and melody by
  Jon Gailmor

Love—by the Water: No. 1 – Blow the Candles Out (1997, 3:30)
  ECS#5249, SATB, piano

Love—by the Water: No. 2 – Fare Thee Well (1997, 4:30) ECS#5250,
  SATB, piano

Love—by the Water: No. 3 – Banks of the Ohio (1997, 5:30)
  ECS#5251, SATB, piano (traditional texts adapted by the
  composer)

My Love Walks in Velvet (1978, 4:30) ECS#4312, SATB, piano, text
  by Gwyneth Walker

Now Let Us Sing (2003, 3:30) ECS#6600, SATB, piano, traditional
  text (adapted by the composer)

Ring Out, Wild Bells (2006, 4:00) GW, SATB, piano, text by Alfred,
Lord Tennyson (adapted by the composer)

Sing On! (A Musical Toast) (2003, 3:00) ECS#6524, SATB, piano,
text by Colonel Henry Heveningham

Tell the Earth to Shake (2004, 4:15) ECS#6423, SATB, piano, text by
Thomas Merton

The Dreamers of Dreams (2003, 4:00) ECS#6291, SATB, piano, text
by Arthur O'Shaughnessy

The Road to Freedom (2003, 4:00) ECS#6036, SATB, piano,
traditional text (adapted by the composer)

The Writings on the Wall (1998, 7:30) GW, SATB, piano, texts from
Berlin Wall inscriptions

This Is the Day the Lord Hath Made (1985, 4:30) ECS#4314, SATB,
soprano/bass soli, piano, text by Isaac Watts and Gerard Manley
Hopkins

Three Days by the Sea: No. 1 – The Bottom of the Sea (2004, 3:00)
ECS#6570, SATB, piano

Three Days by the Sea: No. 2 – Gifts from the Sea (2004, 3:30)
ECS#6571, SATB, piano

Three Days by the Sea: No. 3 – Down to the Sea (2004, 5:00)
ECS#6572, SATB, piano, texts by Thomas Merton, Anne
Morrow Lindbergh, and Norah Mary Holland

Three Songs in Celebration of the Family Farm (1988, 13:00) GW,
SATB, piano, texts by Martha Holden

Two Songs: No. 1 – Spring! (1993, 2:30) ECS#5045, SATB, piano

Two Songs: No. 2 – I Carry Your Heart (1993, 2:30) ECS#5067,
SATB, piano, texts by E. E. Cummings

White Horses (1979, 3:30) ECS#4548, SATB, piano, text by E. E.
Cummings

Mixed Chorus with Organ Accompaniment:

A Song of Praise (2003, 3:45) ECS#6286, SATB, organ, text by Isaac
Watts (adapted by the composer)

Dazzling as the Sun (2004, 3:30) ECS#6513, SATB, organ, text by
    Delores Dufner, OSB

Ever with Me (2004, 3:00) ECS#6346, SATB, organ/piano, text from
    Sarum Primer and the Psalms (adapted by the composer)

Faith Grows (2005, 4:00) GW, adult choir–SATB, youth choir, organ,
    text by Frances Wile

God Speaks to Each of Us (1999, 3:00) ECS#5664, SATB, organ, text
    by Rainer Maria Rilke

Love Unfolding (2001, 4:00) ECS#5947, SATB, organ or brass quintet,
    full brass score (ECS#5948) and brass parts (ECS#5949) are also
    available, text by Julian of Norwich

My Beloved Son (2006, 7:00) GW, SATB, solo mezzo-soprano, organ,
    texts by Charles Wesley and Hildegard von Bingen, translated by
    Christopher Brunelle

O *Gracious Light* from *Bethesda Evensong* (1988) ECS#4476, SATB,
    organ, traditional text

Psalm 23 (1998, 3:15) ECS#5374, SATB, organ, text from the Bible

Quiet Wonder (2001, 3:00) ECS#5851, SATB, organ, text by
    Gwyneth Walker

St. John's Trilogy (1990) ECS#4699, congregation, optional SATB
    chorus, organ, texts from the Episcopal Eucharist Service, Rite II

With Thee That I May Live (1997, 5:45) ECS#5277, SATB (children's
    choir, organ, brass quartet, timpani) full score (ECS#5278),
    children's chorus part (ECS#5279), and brass parts (ECS#5280)
    are also available, text by Anna Barbauld and Isaac Watts

Mixed Chorus with Other Instrumental Accompaniment (Solo or Ensemble):

Acquaintance with Nature (2002, 15:00) GW, SATB, clarinet, piano,
    texts by Henry David Thoreau

American Ballads: No. 1 – Lonesome Traveler (1992, 4:45) ECS#4930,
    SATB, SATB soli, flute

American Ballads: No. 2 – Come All Ye Fair and Tender Ladies (1992, 3:40) ECS#4931, SSATBB, flute

American Ballads: No. 3 – Careless Love (1992, 3:40) ECS#4932, SSAA, SSA soli

American Ballads: No. 4 – Clementine (1992, 5:40) ECS#4933, TTBB, TBB soli, flute

American Ballads: No. 5 – Shenandoah (1992, 4:45) ECS#4934, SSAATTBB, flute, traditional texts

Appalachian Carols: No. 1 – Wondrous Love (1998, 4:30) ECS#5666, SATB, brass quintet or piano

Appalachian Carols: No. 2 – Cherry Tree Carol (1998, 5:00) ECS#5667, SATB, brass quintet or piano

Appalachian Carols: No. 3 – Jesus, Jesus Rest Your Head (1998, 3:20) ECS#5668, SATB, brass quintet or piano

Appalachian Carols: No. 4 – Go Tell It on the Mountain (1998, 4:00) ECS#5669 SATB, brass quintet or piano, full brass score (ECS#5665) and brass parts (ECS#5665A) are also available, traditional texts

Be Our Light in the Darkness (from *Bethesda Evensong*) (1988) ECS#4480, SATB, treble solo, organ, percussion, traditional text

Dreams and Dances: No. 1 – Bones, Be Good! (1992, 2:50) ECS#5029, SATB, piano or strings

Dreams and Dances: No. 2 – Some Dreams Hang in the Air (1992, 4:00) ECS#5030, SATB, piano or strings

Dreams and Dances: No. 3 – Let There Be New Flowering (1992, 3:30) ECS#5031, SATB, piano or strings, version for string orchestra available on rental, texts by Lucille Clifton

Every Life Shall Be a Song (2005, 3:00) GW, SATB, piano, John Addington Symonds (adapted by the composer) version for brass quintet, percussion, and keyboard available for sale

Let Freedom Ring! (1995, 10:00) GW, SATB, narrator and concert band, based on the speech, "I Have a Dream" of Martin Luther King

Love Flows from God (2004, 14:00) #6751, SATB (treble voices, brass
quintet, percussion, organ), full score, ECS#6752, parts
ECS#6753, text by Mechtild of Magdeburg (adapted by the
composer)

Love Unfolding (2001, 4:00) ECS#5947, SATB, organ or brass quintet,
full brass score (ECS#5948) and brass parts (ECS#5949) also
available, text by Julian of Norwich

New Millennium Suite: No. 1 – Sinner Man (1999–2000, 4:30) #5865,
SATB, piano

New Millennium Suite: No. 2 – Peace, I Ask of Thee, O River
(1999–2000, 4:30) #5866, SATB, piano

New Millennium Suite: No. 3 – Down by the Riverside (1999–2000,
4:30) #5867, SATB, piano, version for brass quintet, percussion,
and keyboard available for sale, traditional texts

Now Let Us Sing (2003, 3:30) ECS#6600, SATB, piano, traditional
text (adapted by the composer), version for brass quintet,
percussion, and keyboard available for sale

Rejoice!—Christmas Songs (2001, 11:00) ECS#6067, SATB,
piano/organ, version for brass quintet, percussion (two), and
keyboard available, full score (ECS#6633) and parts (ECS#6634)
available, texts by William Chatterton Dix, John Mason Neale,
and Christina Rossetti (adapted by the composer)

Sweet Molly and Friends (1998, 10:00) GW, SATB, tuba, traditional
texts

The Golden Harp (1999, 30:00) SATB chorus and string quartet (full
score and string parts for sale from MMB; choral scores for rental
or sale from MMB) text by Rabindranath Tagore

The Rose, the Briar, and the Bicycle (2002, 10:30) ECS#6208, SATB,
oboe, piano, oboe part (#6209) available, traditional texts

Together in Song (2005, 13:10) ECS#6761, SATB, brass quintet,
percussion, piano, full score (#6762) and parts (#6763) are
available, traditional texts (adapted by the composer)

With Thee That I May Live (1997, 5:45) ECS#5277, SATB, children's choir, organ, brass quartet, timpani, full score (ECS#5278), children's chorus part (ECS#5279), and brass parts (ECS#5280) also available, text by Anna Barbauld and Isaac Watts

Mixed Chorus with Orchestral Accompaniment (Keyboard Reductions Available):

Come Life, Shaker Life! (2001, 30:00) GW, SATB, children's chorus, piano, version for orchestra available (traditional texts adapted by the composer)

Crossing the Bar (2004, 3:30) ECS#6378, SATB, piano, version for orchestra available, score ECS#6375, parts ECS#6376, text by Alfred, Lord Tennyson

The Golden Harp (1999, 30:00) SATB chorus and string orchestra, texts by Rabindranath Tagore

I Will Be Earth (1992, 2:30) #4887, SSATB, piano, version for chamber orchestra available, score ECS#6538, parts ECS#6539, text by May Swenson

New Millennium Suite: No. 1 – Sinner Man (1999–2000, 4:30) #5865, SATB, piano)

New Millennium Suite: No. 2 – Peace, I Ask of Thee, O River (1999–2000, 4:30) #5866 (SATB, piano)

New Millennium Suite: No. 3 – Down by the Riverside (1999–2000, 4:30) #5867, SATB, piano, version for orchestra available on rental, second movement scored for string orchestra alone, full score #5868, parts rental #5868a, traditional texts

River Songs: No. 1 – Deep River (1996, 6:30) #5383, SATB, piano

River Songs: No. 2 – A Mule Named Sal (1996, 5:00) #5384, SATB, piano

River Songs: No. 3 – The Water Is Wide (1996, 8:00) #5385, SATB, piano, version for chamber orchestra available on rental, traditional texts

Rejoice!—Christmas Songs (2001, 11:00) ECS#6067, SATB, piano/organ, version for orchestra available, full score (ECS#6068) and parts (ECS#6069) available, texts by William Chatterton Dix, John Mason Neale, and Christina Rossetti (adapted by the composer)

To an Isle in the Water: No 1. – The Lake Isle of Innisfree (2005, 4:15) ECS#6708, SATB, piano

To an Isle in the Water: No 2. – Shy One (2005, 3:45) ECS#6709, SATB, piano

To an Isle in the Water: No 3. – When You Are Old (2005, 3:30) ECS#6710, SATB, piano

To an Isle in the Water: No 4. – Song of Wandering Aengus (2005, 4:15) ECS#6711, SATB, piano, version for chamber orchestra available, full score (ECS#6712) and parts (ECS#6713) available, texts by W. B. Yeats

Women's Chorus Unaccompanied:

Hebrides Lullaby (1996, 3:45) ECS#5263, SSA, traditional text

My Girls: No. 1 – This Morning (1998, 3:00) #TC-151, SSA

My Girls: No. 2 – To My Girls (1998, 2:30) #TC-152, SSA

My Girls: No. 3 – Sisters (1998, 3:40) #TC-153, SSA, texts by Lucille Clifton

The Spirit of Women: 1. So Many Angels! (2000, 3:40) ECS#6184, SSA

The Spirit of Women: 2. Walk That Valley (2002, 3:15) ECS#6185, SSAA

The Spirit of Women: 3. Never Sit Down! (2002, 3:45) ECS#6186, SSAA, traditional texts

Women's Chorus with Piano Accompaniment:

Bones, Be Good! (1992, 2:50) ECS#6561, SSA, piano, text by Lucille Clifton

Crossing the Bar (2004, 3:30) ECS#6377, SSAA, piano, text by Alfred, Lord Tennyson

Gifts from the Sea (2006, 3:30) #6717, SSAA, piano, text by Anne Morrow Lindbergh

How Can I Keep from Singing? (1999, 3:30) ECS#5655, SSA, piano, traditional text, Quaker hymn

I Thank You God (1998, 4:00) ECS#5331, SSA, piano, text by E. E. Cummings

Let Evening Come (2001, 3:30) ECS#5946, SSA, piano, text by Jane Kenyon

My Love Walks in Velvet (1978, 1999, 4:30) ECS#5663, SSA, piano, text by Gwyneth Walker

Now I Become Myself (1999, 4:00) ECS#5409, SSA, piano, text by May Sarton

Now Let Us Sing! (2004, 3:30) ECS#6601, SSAA, piano, traditional text (adapted by the composer)

Peace I Ask of Thee, O River (2005, 4:30) ECS#6550, SSAA, piano, traditional text

Songs for Women's Voices: No. 1 – Women Should Be Pedestals (1993, 2:15) ECS#5020, SSA, piano

Songs for Women's Voices: No. 2 – Mornings Innocent (1993, 2:30) ECS#5021, SSAA, piano

Songs for Women's Voices: No. 3 – The Name Is Changeless (1993, 1:15) ECS#5022, SSA

Songs for Women's Voices: No. 4 – Love Is a Rain of Diamonds (1993, 2:45), ECS#5023, SSA, piano

Songs for Women's Voices: No. 5 – In Autumn (1993, 3:20) ECS#5024, SSA, soprano and alto soli, piano)

Songs for Women's Voices: No. 6 – I Will Be Earth (1993, 2:30) ECS#5025, SSA, piano, texts by May Swenson

The Silver Apples of the Moon (1986, 2:45) ECS#4313, SSA, piano, text by William Butler Yeats

The Tree of Peace (2002, 5:30) ECS#6463, SSAA, piano, text by John Greenleaf Whittier (adapted by the composer)

The Whole World (in His Hands) (1999, 4:30) ECS#6228, treble
voices, piano, traditional text

To Sing Is to Fly (2003, 2:30) GW, SSAA, piano, text by Joan Baez

Words of Strength (2004, 5:00) ECS#6680, women's chorus (SSA),
girls' chorus (SA), piano, girls' chorus part available (#6681)
(traditional text adapted by the composer)

Women's Chorus with Organ Accompaniment:

Magnificat (from *Bethesda Evensong*) (1988) ECS#4477, SSAA, solo
mezzo-soprano, organ, traditional text

The Lord's Prayer (from *Bethesda Evensong*) (1988) ECS#4479, SSA,
organ, text from the Bible (The Lord's Prayer)

Women's Chorus with Orchestral Accompaniment:

Crossing the Bar (2004, 3:30) ECS#6377, SSAA, piano, version for
orchestra available, score ECS#6374, parts ECS#6376, text by
Alfred, Lord Tennyson

How Can I Keep from Singing? (2004, 3:30) #5100, SSAA, piano,
version for chamber orchestra available, full scores available
for sale: SATB (#6337), SSAA (#6342), and TTBB (#6343),
traditional text (Quaker hymn)

I Thank You God (1998, 4:00) ECS#5331, SSA, piano, version for
chamber orchestra available, score ECS#6595, parts ECS#6596,
text by E. E. Cummings

Peace I Ask of Thee, O River (2005, 4:30) ECS#6550, SSAA, piano,
version for string orchestra available, score ECS#6551, parts
ECS#6552, traditional text

Songs for Women's Voices: No. 1 – Women Should Be Pedestals (1993,
2:15) ECS#5020, SSA, piano

Songs for Women's Voices: No. 2 – Mornings Innocent (1993, 2:30)
ECS#5021, SSAA, piano

Songs for Women's Voices: No. 3 – The Name Is Changeless (1993,
1:15) ECS#5022, SSA

Songs for Women's Voices: No. 4 – Love Is a Rain of Diamonds (1993, 2:45) ECS#5023, SSA, piano

Songs for Women's Voices: No. 5 – In Autumn (1993, 3:20) ECS#5024, SSA, soprano and alto soli, piano

Songs for Women's Voices: No. 6 – I Will Be Earth (1993, 2:30) ECS#5025, SSA, piano, version for chamber orchestra available for sale from ECS Publishing, texts by May Swenson

Men's Chorus:

American Ballads: No. 4 – Clementine (1992, 5:40) #4933, TTBB, TBB soli, flute, traditional text

How Can I Keep From Singing? (2004, 3:30) TTBB, piano, version for chamber orchestra available, traditional text (Quaker hymn)

Love Was My Lord and King!: No. 1 – A Sentinel (2003, 3:45) ECS#6371, TTBB, piano

Love Was My Lord and King!: No. 2 – There Rolls the Deep (2003, 3:45), ECS#6372, TTBB, piano

Love Was My Lord and King!: No. 3 – Crossing the Bar (2003, 3:30) ECS#6373, TTBB, piano, version for orchestra available, score #6369, parts #6370, texts by Alfred, Lord Tennyson